First published in Great Britain in 2007 by
Moot Community Publishing
St Matthew's, Westminster
St Matthew's House
20 Great Peter Street
London SW1P 2BU
www.moot.uk.net

1

A catalogue record for this book is available from
the British Library

ISBN 978-0-9559800-0-8

Printed in Great Britain by Lulu.com

Typeset by Gareth Powell
Cover design and illustrations by Gareth Powell

Contents

You can download each of the appendices from the Moot Grey Space at www.moot.uk.net

Background

For sometime I have been involved in what started out as alternative worship which became emerging forms of church and most recently has become labelled 'Fresh Expressions' of church. Throughout this period (now most of my adult life from the age of nineteen) I have seen this loose movement grow with few resources, little encouragement, and challenging contexts. I still believe these forms of church reveal something of God, yes messy, inconsistent, and still discerning a voice in a culture of exile, but a significant voice none-the-less.

This work seeks to explore the social and theological significance of the more Anglican emerging/fresh expressions of Church in the UK context, although drawing on one American emerging church project. It seeks to discern and understand the voice of Anglican emerging church practitioners about how they understand the significance of the emerging church in a growing post-secular and post-modern contemporary culture. Why Anglican? Well because many of the Alt/Emerging/Fresh Expressions have come from some connection with Anglicanism. People may not have noticed, but there is a quiet revolution going on in the Church of England at the moment, one where emerging churches only a few years ago were seen as the eccentric fringe, but now find themselves as a key focus of Church policy and practice concerning contextual mission.

As a piece of pioneering research, this study brings fresh thinking and analysis in a somewhat neglected area of ecclesiology. It is hoped that others will pick up the many unanswered questions that this study evokes.

The source material and appendices to this study can be accessed through the 'Moot Grey Space', see www.moot.uk.net.

Ian Mobsby, Priest Missioner to the Moot Community, Associate Missioner of the Fresh Expressions Team and Associate Lecturer to the St Pauls Theological Centre, Holy Trinity Brompton, London.
December 2006.

Acknowledgements

This book and dissertation is the result of the excellent work and commitment of the four study church projects, namely 'B1' Birmingham, 'Sanctus 1' Manchester, 'COTA' Seattle, and my own home church project, 'Moot' in London.

I am especially grateful to those who participated and contributed in the group narrative research that included Ian Carrington, Vicki Camfield, Laura Drane, Ben Edson, Craig Gilman, Geoff Lanham, Gwen Owen, Gareth Powell, Carey Radcliffe, Mike Radcliffe, Graham Richards, Karen Ward and Phil Woodward.

In the complex transcription process of this project, my thanks go to my mum Jacqueline Mobsby for her clerical support. My thanks go to Simeon Barnes and Lizzie Everard for their inadvertent support with trialling the original 'NAOMIE VC' questions whose verbal feedback assisted in early modifications.

In the various write-up phases of this dissertation, my thanks go to Danielle Welch, Jonathan Bartley, Jonathan Mosedale and the Revd Paul Bayes for their proofing feedback.

My particular thanks go to my final year tutor and research supervisor Dr Malcolm Brown, who has supported and guided me through not only this MA research dissertation, but also through my ordination training.

Thanks also to Sion College London, and the Church of the Apostles Seattle, for their financial support for the data collection phase of this project, and to my training incumbent, the Revd Philip Chester at St Matthews Westminster, for the time to complete the research and write-up of this study.

Finally I would like to acknowledge the encouragement of Geoff Plant who kept me going with this study when I was finding my work/study balance extremely challenging.

Chapter One

Introduction

In the last twenty years the Church of England has increasingly recognised the contribution of 'new forms of Church' in its ongoing mission. At the time of writing this study, there were examples of Anglican 'new forms of church' happening in a number of other Anglican provinces including the United States, Australia and Canada. In the past, 'mission activities' and 'church' have been separated out; where 'doing mission' was seen as an activity that was largely about supporting overseas initiatives often within countries of the former British Empire and 'two-thirds world'.[1] Lately however, there has been increased awareness that the Church should be more involved in contemporary and contextual forms of mission.[2] In an important Church of England report called 'Breaking new Ground'[3] concerned with mission to England in 1994, this separation between 'being church' and 'doing mission' was challenged. The report promoted the need to experiment with more missionary focused forms of church, and argued that the parish system of church as "one-size-fits-all" was insufficient to meet this need.[4] The report highlighted the need for network forms of church (that reflect non-geographical relational connection) to work along side parish churches.

In a more recent report, this theme of the 'experimental' working alongside the traditional has been called a 'mixed economy' of Church - expressing the expectation that such 'fresh expressions of church' should work collaboratively within Anglican Church structures.[5] This new report entitled the 'Mission-Shaped Church' — the result of a national working group led by the current Bishop of Maidstone, Graham Cray — sought to give such 'fresh' or 'experimental' expressions of church a theological framework, and to legitimise them as authentic 'missionary-focused churches'.[6] In particular it recognised twelve experimental groupings as 'fresh expressions' of Anglican church.[7]

- Alternative worship communities
- Base Ecclesial Communities
- Café church
- Cell church
- Churches arising out of community initiatives (both out of community projects, and the restructuring or refounding of an existing church to serve a community)
- Multiple and midweek congregations
- Network-focused churches (churches connecting with

specific networks)

- School-based and school-linked congregations and churches
- Seeker church
- Traditional church plants
- Traditional forms of church inspiring new interest (including new monastic communities)
- Youth congregations

The report stated that such churches contributed to the important activity of trying to narrow the growing gap between church and culture. The report passed through the General Synod and has become a central policy of the Church of England. Additionally, Dr Rowan Williams, the current Archbishop of Canterbury, has stated that the development of 'fresh expressions of church' is a key initiative of his primacy.[5] Accordingly the Lambeth Partners[8] have funded an Archbishop's Missioner and a small agency to promote the development of 'fresh expressions of church' throughout the Church of England.[9] The Archbishop has stated:[10]

> At present, we stand at a watershed in the life of the Church of England - not primarily because of the controversies that have been racking us, but because we have to ask whether we are capable of moving towards a more 'mixed economy' - recognising church where it appears and having the willingness and the skill to work with it. Mission, it's been said, is finding out what God is doing and joining in. And at present there is actually an extraordinary amount going on in terms of the creation of new styles of church life. We can call it church planting, 'new ways of being church' or various other things; but the point is that more and more patterns of worship and shared life are appearing on the edge of our mainstream life that cry out for our support, understanding and nurture if they are not to get isolated and unaccountable.

At about the time the Mission Shaped Church research was being carried out, another working group, chaired by Professor Toyne, was looking at the legal issues involved, and in particular the provisions of the 'pastoral measure' that govern what is legitimately church. A report entitled 'A Measure for Measures' was produced which sought to clarify how a traditionally defined parish church may work with 'non-geographically defined' forms such as 'network' churches.[11] The report raised certain expectations that non-geographically defined churches needed to meet if they were to be recognised as being authentically Anglican in Church law:[12]

(i)   They should not undermine the virtues of the parochial system and should not threaten the different integrities of the Church of England.

(ii)   They should include provision for a minister licensed and accredited by the Bishop but should not be defined by reference to a person.

(iii)   They should include a distinctively Anglican component.

(iv)   They should normally be within synodical government structures;

(v)   They should, ideally, be mutually supportive with surrounding parishes;

(vi)   It should if necessary be possible to establish such arrangements without the consent of existing incumbents or parishes, subject to consideration of their representations.

However, the report acknowledges that it is extremely difficult to define how a particular church may prove to be 'distinctively Anglican' and there is no attempt made at any stage in the report to define what this may mean despite the inclusion of a detailed theological section.

By contrast, the Cray report does (albeit briefly) explore Anglican ecclesiology and fresh expressions of church, with some expectations regarding how they are distinctively Anglican with reference to church law, church practice, and belonging to diocesan structures with a vision of unity in diversity. Helpfully the report states:

> Engagement in the dynamics of its theological and practical formation
> is one of the distinctive features of the Church in Anglicanism:
> there is no straightforward 'doctrine of the Church' but an ongoing
> theological formation of church life.[13]

The report goes further, stating that fresh expressions of church are associated with change, but does not go into the practical detail about how the tension between being 'distinctively Anglican' and being a 'fresh expression of church' centred on change may be resolved.[14]

Despite the limited exploration of what 'being Anglican' means in practice, both the Toyne and Cray reports give detailed theological analysis of what 'being Church' is, and in particular what being a 'missionary Church' is.

Regarding what is 'legally church', the Toyne report recommended legal amendments to the current pastoral measure of the Church of England.[15] General Synod endorsed the report, and a further legal working group is formulating a new pastoral measure that will come into effect in approximately 2008.

Although significant progress has been made to legitimise 'fresh expressions of church', questions remain (particularly from those in traditional settings) about experimental forms of church, as to both their necessity and their nature as 'really Anglican'. Arguably, some from within established Anglican Churches have resisted supporting such initiatives, both politically and financially.

Methodology

This study seeks to select four examples of Anglican 'fresh expressions' of Church, three in England and one in the USA,[16] and through set criteria, to explore why they were created, what drives them, how they define themselves and what their vision is; and to test them against the questions raised in the Church of England 'Toyne report', specifically concerning how they are being legitimately 'church' and legitimately 'Anglican'. This study will look further to where they agree, disagree, and how they are getting on with doing what they set out to do.

Before commencing the interviews with the project-groups, the author completed an extensive review of the literature pertaining to 'fresh' and 'emerging' forms of church, the meaning of 'Anglicanism', and social and theological understandings of 'church'.

Following this, a 'participatory action' 'case-study' model of research was chosen, given the strength of this approach to identify narrative data,[17] that could be used to explore the study question in conjunction with the reviewed literature. As has been said:

> A primary reason for using participative action research is to take part in a social innovation, not just testing or reformulating theoretical propositions or ideas. A great deal of learning in such projects will involve conditions for creating and disseminating innovations. Thus, in addition to being concerned with evaluation, the researcher will be interested in studying focuses that lead to change.[18]

In a similar study, Jamieson found the following strength in this form of methodology:

> Using a face-to-face interviewing method allows for questioning in much greater detail than is possible in a written or telephone survey because these interviews were primarily conducted in the interviewees' homes in a relaxed conversational manner I was able to pick up on the hesitations, gestures and underlying feelings of the interviewees and explore these for a richer understanding of experience and faith journey.[19]

Such a methodology is following a 'biological' case study approach, which is understood to be:

> A research method, a way of finding out more about some aspect of reality through a very detailed analysis.[20]

It is biological because it seeks to establish 'concepts and contexts', 'systems of ideas' and 'ways to view the world'. Biological approaches to case-study research have been proven to work well in situations of organisational change, product development, and fashion.[21]

However there are some limitations in collecting such forms of 'qualitative data'.

> The data-gathering technique is the subjectivity of the researcher, the unsystematic gathering of data, reliance on subjective measurement,

and possible distortion of the observed behaviour.[22]

The data therefore has set limitations and cannot be used for statistical purposes.[23] The weakness of using the author researching his own 'fresh expression of church' project as a sample group is recognised, in that it may distort the source narrative data and results.[24] However, as Cole has stated, this form of participatory research may actually be a strength rather than a weakness to enable detailed and relevant questions to elicit more accurate data.[25]

> I would stress that the participant observation role, as others have observed, allowed me to understand the kind of questions that needed answering. Standard research approaches often assume that the researcher knows the important questions to be asked. Moreover, the activist role allowed me access to a wide range of organisational activities that is seldom possible under the more traditional passive participant observer role.[26]

To further limit the possible distortion of the involvement of the author, the "NAOMIE" form of project evaluation that had a proven track record in participatory action research with youth work and other voluntary organisation narrative research was chosen as a framework for the interviews.[27] This process promotes a consistency of approach between interviews and can therefore act to limit the potential distorting effects of the author's own views. The "NAOMIE" form of project evaluation has been adapted by Brown and those he worked with, to include two further categories to include aspects concerning 'values' and 'church involvement', so that the 'NAOMIE' became the 'NAOMIE VC' process. This process then covers the following areas:[28]

1. What is/was the NEED of members?, of the group? Of others and WHY?

2. What do/did we AIM to do about this? What do we/did we want to go? Where do we want to go/where did we go? WHY?

3. What specific OBJECTIVES can/did we set? What will others be able to do as a result? How will/was effectiveness measured?

4. What is/was the best METHOD to achieve the desired results?

5. How do/did we IMPLEMENT the plan?

6. How do/did we EVALUATE the plan? Did we meet the objectives? What went well? What difficulties occurred? What could be learned for the future? What new needs exist?

Then with the additional areas:[29]

7. What were/are the VALUES?
8. What was/is the CHURCH INVOLVEMENT?

Specific questions were then formulated to meet this process, which were taken to research supervision before beginning the interviews.[30] This approach then offered the advantages of participative action research combined with the 'NAOMIE VC' process creating a form of detailed data collection and consistency between interviews.

Using the typology set by Langrish, the sample selection was set against a combination of 'known best practice'[31], 'ease of access' or 'the ones next door'[32] and 'taxonomic' criteria[33], created and agreed before considering potential projects.[34]

1. Consider themselves as having some connection with Anglicanism.
2. A group that falls into the 'group type' definitions of the 'Mission-Shaped Church' report. The group could be an autonomous project or a church or part of a church.
3. Longevity – is a project that is likely not to end during the survey stages of this study.
4. Accessibility – have a proven track record regarding communications to be able to respond to the data gathering elements of this study.
5. Differing geographical areas – reflecting different contexts.
6. Have a reputation for excellence in practice and exhibit a variety of differing activities to reflect the needs of the particular project-users.
7. The Group and Group leaders are willing to participate in the 'NAOMIE' process.
8. That the groups have responded in writing that they are happy to participate in the 'NAOMIE' process by email or letter.

These criteria therefore fulfil the three identified Langrish sample selection areas for a biological case-study research method:

- 'Known best practice' – question 6.
- 'Ease of access' – question 3 and 4.
- 'Taxonomic' – questions 1,2,5,7,8.

A number of projects met all the set criteria reflecting the above three Langrish typology definitions. Of these, four groups agreed to participate in the research:

- 'Church of the Apostles', Episcopal Church of the United States of America, Diocese of Olympia, Fremont, Seattle, USA.
- 'Sanctus 1', Church of England, Diocese of Manchester, England.
- 'B1', Church of England, Diocese of Birmingham, England.
- 'Moot', Church of England, Diocese of London, England.

The leaders of these four groups were then approached to clarify whether they would participate in formal recorded interviews. These leaders were:

1. Revd Karen Ward, Church of the Apostles, Diocese of Olympia, Episcopal Church of the United States of America.
2. Captain Ben Edson, Church Army Officer, Sanctus 1, Diocese of Manchester, Church of England.
3. Revd Geoff Lanham, B1, Diocese of Birmingham, Church of England.
4. Gareth Powell (lead representative for Moot for the research interviews and discussions), Moot, St Matthews Westminster, Diocese of London, Church of England.

Each leader then went back to their church project forums, where at least two members of each project and their leader would participate in formal interviews. At this stage each participant was sent a written explanation of the process, and was asked to give consent for participation, and for the recording and transcription of research material.[35] At the interview stage, the researcher assisted setting up an activity or event as a 'group member' on average for one day, in addition to completing the recorded interviews and attending an act of Christian worship. Following this, the recordings were professionally transcribed, and checked for accuracy by each member of the interview groups. Finally the Internet and a piece of software called "MSN Messenger" were utilised for an online discussion between all the leaders of the project groups to clarify unclear content of the interviews. As the transcript offer unique source data for this study, they have been included in the appendices. The transcripts narrative source data and related reviewed literature will be used to explore four key questions that taken together answer the study question.

Chapter 2, "What do people mean by fresh expressions of church?"
Chapter 3, "Why do we need new forms of church?"
Chapter 4, "What makes these new forms church?"
Chapter 5, 'What makes these new forms Anglican?"

In Chapter 6, the conclusion, will include content on the following:

- The main points that have emerged from the study.
- A comment on the ability of the proposed reform of the 'Pastoral Measure' to act as a tool to define what is legitimately Anglican.
- A comment on the material of the 'Mission-Shaped Church' report and whether it assists the Church to clarify and address issues concerning new forms of Church.
- Finally areas or questions for further research coming out of this study will be highlighted.

Brief background on the groups and author

B1 began as a 'network church plant' in the Anglican Diocese of Birmingham drawing people mainly from the south area of the city. Its current full-time and paid minister was previously the assistant vicar of the sending church. Its focus is described as 'being church in central Birmingham's B1 postcode area'. Currently it hosts various mission and experimental forms of worship in a variety of settings from bars and pubs to hotels and health spa clinics. The church currently has a core group of around 52 adults and 23 children, with an average of 40 people attending worship services. Events include discussion or spiritual enquiry groups, spirituality groups, film discussion, book groups, music nights, and social gatherings. 'B1' is known as a 'network church' utilising alternative worship.

Sanctus 1 began as a joint mission initiative between the Church Army and Manchester

Diocese as a response to the assessed spiritual needs of Manchester City centre in September of 2001. At this point a fulltime, paid Church Army Officer was commissioned as a facilitator. This quickly led to the formation of a networked focused 'fresh expression of church' that ran artistic-driven mission activities such as DJ nights, late night café church events, alternative worship services and participation in new age film nights and art fairs. Recently, the group has grown into a Methodist/Anglican ecumenical project, and a paid full time Methodist minister has joined the team. Currently the core group is around 55 people, with around 50 attending services and events. 'Sanctus 1' is highly regarded as a leading 'fresh expression of church' project, being a combination of a 'late night' café church, network church and alternative worship community.

Moot began in January 2003 as a specifically alternative worship community based in Westminster, central London where people travelled in from various parts of the city to form a network-relational community. From this initial act of worship, the group expanded to run discussion groups, scriptural explorations, parties and other gatherings as an attempt to pattern a spiritual way of life in a postmodern urban culture. In June 2004 the author, under the initiative of the Bishop of London, was ordained to serve a non-stipendiary title (2.5 days a week) to St Matthew's Church Westminster, and the Moot Community, to facilitate development as a 'fresh expression of church'. Currently the core group is around 20, with on average 30 to 40 attending services and events. The group seek to develop more 'spirituality and arts as mission' activities and a spiritual rhythm of life to sustain the community. Moot is seen as a leading 'fresh expression of church' project being a combination of a 'network church and alternative worship community'.

Church of the Apostles, (COTA) began in 2002, as the initiative of Revd Karen Ward who led an initial group of five people to set up an emerging church café mission in central Seattle. The Church is now an ecumenical partnership in Seattle funded by the Episcopal Diocese of Olympia and the Northwest Washington Synod of the Evangelical Lutheran Church in America. Karen now works full-time, with two other paid staff, to develop music, worship, pastoral care and mission events. The group has run an internet café as a form of Christian presence in the Fremont area of Seattle. The church runs events every day, normally arts related, and have created new forms of liturgy and forms of service drawing on ancient and Anglican resources. Currently the core group is around 100, with on average 40-75 attending services and events. Current activities include;

weekly services, gallery nights, music performance nights, film nights, yoga classes, and café social gatherings. 'COTA' are recognised as a leading 'emerging church' being a combination of 'café church', 'alternative worship community' and 'arts collective'.

The author has a background of experience of being involved in three experimental Church of England forms of church from the 1980s, and is currently serving a title to Moot and St Matthew's Westminster for the Diocese of London in his third year of curacy, as full time Priest Missioner.

Chapter Two

What do people mean by fresh expressions of church?

"Fresh expressions are forms of church that resonate and speak the cultural languages of the current culture, (whatever that is) in order to speak and embody the gospel within that culture. Fresh forms often will critique culture as well as express it ... It's about having the freedom to address the cultural discontinuity between church culture and people's everyday culture."[36]

In all the transcripts[37] for this study, there is much debate about the labels covering 'fresh expressions of church'. This chapter seeks to explore how these responses resonate with the literature available on this subject and ask: What are the sociological understandings of this term? What makes it a distinctive grouping? How does this grouping relate to the idea of a 'mixed economy of Church?' Evidence is then explored concerning the existence of two sub-groupings of fresh expressions labelled 'emerging' and 'inherited' forms and the corresponding functional and theological implications of these groupings.

In the transcripts, every group identified with some of the experimental types of 'fresh expressions of church', which were largely 'alternative worship', 'network church' and 'café church'.[38] However, at the same time, there was a general resistance to or dis-ease with conforming to 'labels'. At best, each project was a combination of a number of the stated experimental types.

Bayes attributes the origins of the term 'fresh expressions of church' in an Anglican context to Bishop Stephen Cottrell, who consciously used it to reflect the Church of England's 'Declaration of Assent'[39] to identify mission at the heart of the Church.

> The Church of England is part of the one, holy, catholic and apostolic Church worshipping the one true God, Father, Son and Holy Spirit. It professes the faith uniquely revealed in the Holy Scriptures and set forth in the catholic creeds, which faith the Church is called upon to proclaim afresh in each generation. Led by the Holy Spirit it has borne witness to Christian truth in its historic formularies, the thirty-nine Articles of Religion, the Book of Common Prayer, and the ordering of Bishops, Priests and Deacons. (Canon C15).

By so doing, he emphasised the need for the church to have confidence in the Christian

Gospel with an explicit call to openness and flexibility in its expression.[39] In other words, an openness to see what will emerge when the gospel is immersed in a particular mission cultural context, 'afresh' every generation.[40] In this way, the form of church will be new, but which relates to the historic tradition.

This focus on the church as 'emerging' from engagement with context (an inherently evolutionary process, as it engages with our western cultural context)[41] is a key focus to what has been called the 'emerging' or 'emergent' church.[42] A quick survey utilising any internet search engine will elicit a plethora of church projects utilising this term around the western post-industrialised nations that include the UK, USA, Canada, Australia, New Zealand, Ireland and other parts of Western Europe.[43] Many of these projects are extremely new, making labels particularly difficult to interpret. As Murray states:

> Emerging churches are so disparate there are exceptions to any generalisations. Most are too new and too fluid to classify, let alone assess their significance. There is no consensus yet about what language to use: 'new ways of being church'; 'emerging church'; 'fresh expressions of church'; 'future church'; 'church next'; or 'the coming church'. The terminology used here contrasts 'inherited' and 'emerging' churches.[44]

Additionally the phrases 'fresh expression of Church' and 'emerging' church are also synonymous with 'fluid' or 'liquid' church used by Pete Ward.[45]

The first use of the phrase 'emerging church' appears to have been used by Larson & Osborne in 1970 in the context of reframing the meaning of 'church' in the latter part of the twentieth century.[46] This book, contains a short vision of the 'emerging church' which has a profoundly contemporary feel in the early twenty-first century, and which resonates strongly with the Mission-shaped Church report and the responses in the transcripts. Larson & Osborne note the following themes:

- Rediscovering contextual & experimental mission in the western church.
- Forms of church that are not restrained by institutional expectations.
- Open to change and God wanting to do a new thing.

- Use of the key word ... "and". Whereas the heady polarities of our day seek to divide us into an either-or camp, the mark of the emerging Church will be its emphasis on both-and. For generations we have divided ourselves into camps: Protestants and Catholics, high church and low, clergy and laity, social activists and personal piety, liberals and conservatives, sacred and secular, instructional and underground.
- It will bring together the most helpful of the old and the best of the new, blending the dynamic of a personal Gospel with the compassion of social concern.
- It will find its ministry being expressed by a whole people, wherein the distinction between clergy and laity will be that of function, not of status or hierarchical division.
- In the emerging Church, due emphasis will be placed on both theological rootage and contemporary experience, on celebration in worship and involvement in social concerns, on faith and feeling, reason and prayer, conversion and continuity, the personal and the conceptual. [46]

More recently, the phrase 'emerging church' was used by Robert Warren in the mid-1990s as a descriptor for the 'building of missionary congregations'.[47] In his writings, Warren challenges the 'emerging church' to explore 'being healthy and contextual church', balancing 'worship, mission and community'. He further challenges the church to explore living out this healthy expression of Christian spirituality in the mission field of our current 'cultural shift' into 'postmodernity'.[48] Warren also coined the term 'inherited church' to describe the form and function of church that was appropriate for the 'Western church' from the enlightenment as the dawn of modernity through to late modernity in the twentieth century. He argued that the 'emerging church' would be the form of church to re-engage with this change of cultural paradigm into postmodernity.[49] By implication Warren argued that postmodernity was a clearly identifiable social phenomenon requiring a significant missionary response from the church.

Reflecting back on this challenge, Murray and Riddell clearly agree with Warren that the 'emerging church' has begun to respond to this need to engage with forms of worship, mission and community that resonate with postmodern culture, by holding it as a 'primary motivation' in the early twenty-first century.[50] So in what way is this grouping of 'fresh expressions of church' distinctive?

Much of the literature pertaining to 'fresh expressions of church' uses the language of attempting to incarnate a corrective response to address the perceived gap between 'inherited' or 'solid' church and postmodern culture.[51]

Before going any further we must briefly explore the implications of postmodernism and postmodernist culture. Farley defines 'postmodernity':

> "As a term for the historical shift, the rise of a new epoch, it names a liberation   into plurality (from provincialisms), relativity (from absolutisms), and difference   (from the old frozen authorities). At the same time it describes the void and anxiety we experience when our very selves are dispersed, beaucratised, isolated, and rendered autonomous."[52]

Many writers contest Warren's 'black and white' understanding of postmodernism.[53] Reading completed by the author indicates that there is unfortunately no single agreed and definitive statement, other than a more typographical response as quoted by Farley. In more philosophical thinking, the term is often used critically of modernism, as the philosophical frame of thinking before 'postmodernism'.[54] In terms of time, 'Postmodernity' suggests a period following modernity, although it is not consistently used in this sense. As a period of time, postmodernity has been described as the culmination of 'postmodern sensibilities'.[55] So changes in worldview – cultural, social and intellectual are a manifestation of the climaxing of postmodern sensibilities. These appear to have been initially articulated as philosophical concerns about the nature and limits of metaphysics, and questions about hermeneutics, subjectivity, otherness, relationships and responsibility.[56] Some writers have expressed particular concern about the relationship between power and authority with the understanding of truth and meta-narratives, which are seen as potentially controlling.[57] All knowledge is seen to be provisional, contextual and subjective.[58] For the purpose of this study, it is assumed that the term 'postmodernism' relates to this set of 'postmodern sensibilities' that include a number of other influences to those outlined above. These include post-structuralist thought[59], post-Christendom values[60], the sociological findings of liquid modernity[61], the socio-cultural effects of the advance of information technology, and the effects of the developing global market as late capitalism (globalisation) on social patterns of behaviour.[62]

Furthermore, for the purpose of this study 'postmodernity' is understood as the epoch of time that is situated at the end of modernity, which can be seen as the either 'late continuation' of modernity (as with Liquid Modernity) or as the time after modernity.[63]

Some theologians such as Milbank have argued that postmodernity, as a critical response to modernity and a refound openness to transcendence, creates the conditions for an opportunity to return to a renewed form of Christendom. He articulates a return to a more enhanced relationship between Church and state reframed in a new context.[64] It is the author's contention that this position is untenable, given the critical approach of general postmodern thinking towards meta-narratives, authority, and power.[65]

Finally, and of great significance, is the link between the global market and forms of political and religious fundamentalism. That the globalising processes create local forms of 'neo-tribal fundamentalist tendencies' as the experience of those on the receiving end.[66] So postmodernism as a concept brings significant threats alongside new possibilities.

We return now to explore the significance of 'fresh expressions of church' in how they relate to postmodern culture.

The Mission-shaped Church report states that 'fresh expressions of church' have reframed their understanding for the biblical term 'ekklesia' from 'congregation' to 'spiritual community'; 'discipleship' has replaced 'attendance'; and 'community' has replaced 'membership'.[67] For Ward, 'community' is further understood as a more fluid network of relationships and communications, rather than necessarily those living in geographical proximity. The 'church community' shifts from being an institution rooted in a place, to a dynamic series of relationships, not necessarily geographically defined.[68] Church events shift from 'church attending' to participation in the body that values difference and diversity.[69] Murray's research shows that many fresh expressions of church endorse the practice of 'belonging before believing', advocating new ways of being community that are more inclusive and avoid defining 'who is in and who is out'.[70] Other writers promote the need for re-engagement in recontextualised forms of symbol, ritual, and liturgy that are less anachronistic to contemporary culture than those in some 'inherited' forms of church.[71]

What is common to the identity of all the projects of this study, is that they developed with very little central planning on behalf of the Diocese[72]. They occurred as the initiative of particular groups wanting to start new contextual church experiments, and are therefore very 'bottom up'. Murray identifies 'emerging churches' beginning in the late 1990s as:

> An apparently spontaneous phenomenon … without central planning, coordination, or consultation. Loose networking, shared stories, 'blogging' on websites and developing friendships were all that connected otherwise isolated initiatives … The churches that have emerged in the past few years have been remarkably diverse ….[73]

> Many emerging churches … were not intended to become churches but developed into churches as those involved found their ecclesiogy transformed by engagement with the community they were serving … They grew into churches as those involved found the culture gap between new Christians and church too wide ….[74]

So to summarise so far, common to any understanding of 'fresh expressions of church' and associated labels, is the sense of being a 'bottom up' experimental church project within one or many of the Mission-shaped Church types, that see their projects as holding to a series of shared values that act as a corrective to the perceived gap between contemporary culture and 'inherited' forms of church. By living out these values, these projects attempt to be contextual forms of church in terms of worship, mission and community in response to the postmodern aspects of current western culture. So what is this shared understanding of western culture and its recent cultural shift that helps people understand what they mean by 'fresh expressions of church'?

Much has been written on our current cultural context, which is too large a subject to adequately describe here. However, there are a number of themes that appear to help 'fresh expressions of church' to understand what and who they are.

Context

Firstly, they are attempting to be church in a culture defined by consumption, pluralism, uncertainty, immediacy, and individuality.[75] This has become so pervasive that many people now define themselves by the clothes they wear, the cars they drive, and the clubs they attend, creating the new 'pick 'n' mix' lifestyle.[76] In a world defined by 'choice' and market economics, much of life has become uncertain and constantly changing. In particular, there is uncertainty in maintaining work that has become more mobile, with higher expenses concerning the cost of living, the cost of housing, higher incidence in divorce and family breakdown, and reduction in free time.[77] Changing technology, particularly developments in communications and computing, have created the global village, which has significantly sped up communications and affected every area of life, so that people have to manage constant flows of information.[78] Life has become fast and fluid.[79] This has in turn created a sense of fragmentation and a constant sense of uncertainty.[80] Social relating has shifted from a sense of place to the network, which as already stated may have no geographical reference point.[81] Regarding 'church going', national figures indicate that attendance figures have been consistently falling,[82] and that many people have stopped attending church altogether, (the dechurched). Recent figures indicate that 40% of the general population are de-churched, 40% are non-churched, (have never attended), and 10% are fringe attenders and 10% are regular attenders.[83] For most people, 'church' is either an utterly foreign culture, or one that they have decided to reject.[84]

Many 'fresh expressions of church' projects understand this context to be the cultural shift from modernity to post or liquid modernity as has been discussed. Whilst some academics in the fields of theology and the humanities doubt the existence of post or liquid modernity as a unique social phenomena, it is clear that most 'fresh expressions of church' understand their social context specifically in terms of post or liquid modernity as defined by Zygmunt Bauman, David Lyon, Anthony Giddens, Manuel Castells and Neil Gaiman, to name but a few.[85] Therefore, 'fresh expressions of church' recognise that the religious life in postmodern times not only demands to be understood differently, but also to be lived differently. How faith finds new forms and how spirituality finds new modes of expression, within postmodern culture, cannot be predicted, and hence church must be experimented with.[86] As Lyon states:

> Traditional religious outlooks, with their fixed points, transcendent anchors, and universal scope, seem out of kilter with the emerging spirit of the age.[87]

Many fresh expressions of church see this post or liquid modern social context as an exciting and positive opportunity for mission, where people appear to be more open to spirituality although not necessarily to traditional forms of Christianity. As Ward states:

> Liquid church, ... starts from the positive elements in the new, fluid environment and tries to work with these and make them part of the way forward for the church ... Only by locating church within culture can we find ways to develop a distinctive Christian expression within that culture.[88]

Some writers have pointed out that the current cultural context, centring on uncertainty and provisionality,[89] has resulted in many people searching for significant forms of spirituality to bring depth, wholeness and connection.[90] Some believe that new technology itself has created a new openness to the impossible as a form of spirituality.[91] This study's project transcripts give many creative and innovative examples of how 'fresh expressions of church' have engaged in contextual mission engaging with this searching for spirituality.[92]

So, in addition to the general understanding of 'fresh expressions of church', many groups also share their understanding of the social context as defined through writings about post and liquid modernity.

This however may be an oversimplification of the actual situation. The term 'cultural shift' used by Warren implies a dynamic point of change, but not necessarily a complete ending of what went before. Change is rarely that dramatic. As Riddell states:

> We live in an age between cultures ... Postmodern times are upon us, which is to say that the old age (modernity) is dying, and the new one (postmodernity) is not wholly apparent as yet. It is one of those transitional times ... when everything is uncertain ....[93]

Caputo supports this complex understanding of our current shifting and increasingly fragmented cultural context, but goes further by stating that it contains elements of the premodern, modern and postmodern co-existing at the same time.[94]

By implication this means that there is a need for contemporary expressions of 'inherited' and 'emerging' forms of church. The Archbishop of Canterbury and the Mission Shaped Church report have called this a 'mixed economy of church', with the traditional co-existing with the experimental.[95] However, it is clear that not all 'emerging churches' agree with the need for this 'mixed economy' or for a role in the continued ministry of more traditional expressions of church.

There are clear voices of dissent, as articulated in the MSN Messenger transcript:

> I think that the major problem with fresh expressions is that nobody really knows what it is. I look on the website and see a vast diversity of churches. This is good but some of them are fairly standard Anglican churches using a tambourine rather than an organ. My concern is that there may be a time when somebody says that the emperor has no clothes on ....[96]

> Big difference for me between emerging church and fresh expressions. Emerging church seems to be more engaging with post-modernity whereas some fresh expressions can be rooted with people still in a culture of modernity.[97]

These comments raise the continuing issue of 'modernity' versus 'postmodernity', and whether postmodernity is a continuous phenomena, part of 'modernity', or whether it is a dramatic point of discontinuity.

The Mission-shaped church report groups church plants and cell churches directly with more emerging forms of church as one list of 'fresh expressions of church'. By so doing it appears to group together two distinctive subgroups into one. This may reflect the need for a mixed economy of 'Fresh Expressions' firstly for less experimental forms of church to reflect more modernist elements of contemporary culture, as well as the more experimental postmodern-focused, in our current 'cultural shift'. It is clear that not everyone agrees with this single grouping of the 'inherited' together with 'emerging' forms of church as 'fresh expressions'. Murray states:

Many [emerging churches] do not regard themselves as church plants; indeed, they distrust the terminology and agenda of church planting.[98]

Brewin goes further to suggest:

> My problem with many of these 'Emerging Church' projects is that they are still attempting to bring church up to date by 'train spotting' some aspects of culture and making church fit it. I want to argue that in the 'Emergent Church' the emphasis will be on being the train, rather than trainspotting: rather than trying to import culture into church and make it 'cool', we need instead to become 'wombs of the divine' and completely rebirth the Church into a host culture ... I think we need to advance with caution for fear of these things precipitating a revolution that will not last, and bringing changes that will just be tactical.[99]

The distinction between various 'fresh expressions of church' appears to relate to the method of contextual theology, (they do or do not employ), and also where the specific project aligns itself as a continuing part of Christendom or post-Christendom.[100] As stated in the same MSN Messenger transcript:

> I think it is also to do with trying to do contextual theology whilst holding onto the ancient traditions of the faith.[101]

Contextual theology takes culture and cultural change seriously and attempts to understand the Christian faith in context,[102] where the language of biblical theology often does not resonate with contemporary experience. Contextual theology has been defined as:

> A way of doing theology in which one takes into account: the spirit and message of the gospel; the tradition of the Christian people; the culture in which one is theologising; and social change in that culture
> ....[103]

It is arguable that many church planting and cell church projects of the late 1990s were examples of specifically conservative evangelical and theologically revivalist 'inherited' churches[104], attune to a more modernist culture, which did not attempt to engage with a postmodern social context or share the values identified above regarding the emerging church.[105] This form of theological engagement conforms to Niebuhr's 'Christ against culture', where 'culture' is seen in negative form, that it may distract people from encountering Christ.[106] It appears that these church plants and cell churches were utilising a model of contextual theology more akin to a 'translation' model where there is emphasis on retaining a Christian identity, (as handed down in the tradition) as more important than cultural identity. There is little awareness or acceptance that the church needs to be immersed in a particular culture in this model.[107] With this form of doing contextual theology, there is often little recognition of the need for church to change, as the view of church is akin to the values of a more Christendom mindset.[108] Related research of experimental forms of church birthed through the House Church movement appears to support this analysis. Walker's study on the outcome of such church experiments, again with revivalist and conservative evangelical theological perspective, found that such experiments proved to be more conservative expressions of the very forms of churches they grew from, which were increasingly more removed from their secular social contexts. He attributed this to a form of church cloning, where each church is a 'microcosm' of the Kingdom being an 'alternative to the dying decaying world'.[109] With such an approach, the gap between church and cultural context remains as wide as with the parent church, if not wider. In so doing, the church's capacity for contextual mission diminishes. As Harvey has stated this form of 'withdrawal' has a profound effect on mission:

> Christian communities must learn to deal with the problems and possibilities posed by life in the "outside" world. But of more importance, any attempt on the part of the church to withdraw from the world would be in effect a denial of its mission.[110]

By contrast, projects operating through a more 'emerging' form of engagement appear to be utilising a synthetic model of contextual theology for a distinctly postmodern context.[111] This model attempts to listen to culture for basic patterns and structures, analyzing culture in order to discover its basic system of symbols. Out of such a "thick description" will emerge basic themes for the local theology. At the same time, however, these themes need to be in dialogue with the basic themes in gospel and tradition, which has a mutually transforming effect.[112] This form of emerging contextual theology holds to a sense of "ancient future" faith worked out with a synthetic model of contextual theology.[113] In this model there is a strong sense that the church needs to be contextual and needs to change, and so is akin to the values of a more post-Christendom mindset.[114] This form of engagement with theology relates to Niebuhr's Synthetic approach, where 'Christ is above culture', but enters into it, where culture is seen in positive terms as it may lead people to Christ.[115]

This variance in contextual theology and mindset concerning Christendom and post-Christendom would explain the difference between cell churches and church plants, and 'emerging' forms of church, and the distrust held by emerging forms of church for the church planting movement.

As well as differences between 'inherited' and 'emerging' forms, Brewin goes further to distinguish between 'emerging' and 'emergent' forms of church.

> Alternative worship [communities] …. [have] elements of emergence in them. However, like many of these activities hailed as part of the emerging church, alternative worship groups are rarely conjunctive organisations, and it seems more likely to me that from my inside view that alternative worship will be seen in the future to have been part of the preparation of the ground for the new to emerge from, rather than the newness itself.[116]

He has articulated his belief that some 'emerging churches' are more akin to 'modernism' than 'postmodernism'. This categorisation is not widely used at the time of writing this study, although it is used by some in the more radical wing of the emerging church.[117] In his analysis, Brewin promotes the use of 'emergent' theory coming out of systems theory and socio-cultural studies, and applies these to the church. Emergent theory stresses the properties of bottom-up, self-starting and sustaining organisational systems drawing on evidence in science and nature.[118] Although not stated directly, the implication of Brewin's writing is that only truly 'emergent' churches can authentically be expressions of a postmodernist social context.[119] So not only do some emerging church projects not measure up, but there is also by implication no place for a 'mixed economy of traditional and emerging church'. This approach remains controversial, but is held by some.

So to conclude this chapter, there appears to be a common understanding about the meaning of "fresh expressions of church" although this terminology is quite new and generalisations are difficult to make. It has a number of synonymous labels, and internationally the phrase "emerging church" is more widely understood. It approximates to a grouping of the experimental typology listed in the Mission Shaped Church report, although there is evidence that few are ever just one of these descriptors and most are a mixture of these forms. There is a strong association with the church's responsibility for mission 'afresh' every generation. There also appears to be a general consensus of understanding regarding the church's role to emerge out of the interplay of engagement with contemporary culture.

However, there also appears to be two distinct sub-groupings of 'fresh expressions of church'. The first appear to be more akin to 'inherited' modes of church, which do not seek to be significantly postmodern in contextual understanding and differ in their model of contextual theology utilising a more 'translation' type approach. This grouping appears to include Cell, Youth and Church Planting new forms. The second is akin to more 'emerging' modes of church which do significantly seek to be postmodern in contextual understanding and use a 'synthetic' model of contextual theology. This grouping appears to include Alternative worship communities, Café churches, and Network churches. Some observers have therefore questioned whether the first grouping of more 'inherited' forms should be listed as being truly 'fresh expressions of church', as these more 'inherited' forms also appear to hold a more Christendom mindset, where more 'emerging' expressions of the experimental typology are committed to new forms of church holding a more post-Christendom mindset and utilising a more 'synthetic' model of contextual theology. However, at the same time, the majority of 'fresh expressions' do accept that we live in a time of cultural shift that implies the need for a mixture of 'inherited' and 'emerging' churches, a concept which has been called 'a mixed economy of church'.

Finally, there has been an additional attempt by Brewin to develop a further classification between 'emerging' and 'emergent' forms of 'fresh expression of church' to relate to this discussion of contextual theology, but this has not yet impacted greatly on the classification or understanding of 'fresh expressions of church'.

Chapter Three

Why do we need new forms of church?

The church in every age needs to rediscover Christ for the culture it finds itself in ... things that are not being renewed/re-freshed will die, to change is to live, to not change is to die. So fresh expressions are not 'an option' just as eating fresh food is not an option to stay healthy and active for the purpose of God's mission ... The church has an 'ancient message' that needs to be fresh in how it is communicated and lived out in any given living culture ....[120]

Building on the explorations in Chapter Two, we must now explore why 'fresh expressions' of church are needed. To do this we need to look back at church history to evaluate how the church has responded to cultural change in the last two millennia. Then we will explore how church relates to culture in general, before exploring to what extent 'inherited forms' of church can (or cannot) relate to postmodern elements of contemporary culture. This will require an exploration of how 'church' as a form of relational community can function in a postmodern context drawing on the concepts of Christendom, post-Christendom, and followed with an exploration of the spirituality that results from postmodernity. Lastly, there will be a short exploration of the four case examples in this study, and the evidence they offer regarding the relationship between 'new forms' of church and postmodern culture.

Drawing on the 'church history of pastoral care', Clebesch and Jaekle identify eight significant epochs, (where there have been points of discontinuity and need for reform), from the early church until the present day. In each of these epochs the church has had to reform in response to socio-cultural and political change.[121] They argue that each new epoch brought new paradigms of thought, values, and understanding of what it means to be human. Following this approach to church history, the church is understood as constantly developing and reforming in response to societal change. If this is the case, then it follows that traditional forms of church are in no way unchanged blueprints of the early church. Furthermore, the gap between the Church and its contextual culture has (by this argument) been a constant source of tension and reform throughout history, as the church attempts to balance the needs of being both contextual and counter-cultural. Although not stated directly, Clebesch and Jaekle hint that we may be now facing a ninth epoch in response to postmodernist changes in thought, values and social behaviour. As explored in chapter two, opinions are divided on whether postmodernism is the beginning of a new epoch to which the church needs to respond. For the purpose of this study, it is assumed that we are currently situated in a 'shifting-point', where elements of the premodern, modern, and, postmodern co-exist. We are left with the questions, 'Can traditional church meet the needs of the postmodern element of contemporary culture?' If not, what form do 'fresh expressions' of church need to take to engage with these new changes in thought, values and understanding of what it means to be human?' To begin, we need to glance at recent statistics in addition to those explored in Chapter Two.

UK Government statistics on religious trends recorded in 2000 are pretty stark:

> Religion is an important part of many people's lives. It involves contact with other individuals and participation in the local community. In 2000, 60 per cent of the population claimed to belong to a specific religion with 55 per cent being Christian. However, half of all adults aged 18 and over who belonged to a religion have never attended a religious service.[122]

Independent long-view statistics appear to support this trend. Particular statistics coming out of the organisation 'Christian Research' predict significant decline in the Church.[123] The following expectations are made for the year 2040 (based on the continuation of current trends):[124]

- Sunday church attendance in the UK may drop to just 2 percent of total population in 2040. This prediction is based on a drastic drop in service attendance in the last decade … there will be a two-thirds drop in attendance in the next 35 years.
- In 2040 almost no one under 20 years of age will attend church, the average attendance age will be 64 years.
- Total membership of all the denominations will fall from 9.4 percent of the population to under 5 percent.
- In 2040 there will be nearly twice as many Muslims at prayer in mosques on Friday as Christians worshipping on Sunday.
- 18,000 more churches will have closed.

The validity of these predictions has been challenged.[125] The Church of England's official statistics drawing on results from 2002/3 identifies a decline from the previous year 2001/2.

The traditional 'usual Sunday attendance' measure showed a drop of two percent to just over 900,000 however provisional figures for 2003 from the Church of England show that more than 1.7 million people attend church and cathedral worship each month while 1.2 million attend each week and one million each Sunday. The ongoing pattern of reduction in numbers of baptisms and confirmations continued in 2003.[126]

Together these results appear to support the evidence stated in Chapter Two of this study: that the church is failing to connect with or appeal to the postmodern elements of our culture. Further, that this significant change in thinking, values and social behaviour warrants the need for 'fresh expressions' to work with more traditional forms of church to meet this gap between church and culture, and that this gap has been created by the current 'shifting-point' into the beginning of a new postmodern epoch.

As well as these statistics, many have asked the question whether traditional and more 'inherited' forms of church can get beyond a 'Christendom' mindset in looking to the current and future need for mission. This holds particular problems for the Church of England as it seeks to explore experimental mission as well as remaining an established national church. In fact the statistics may show the decline of 'Christendom' in the UK context.

Christendom as a concept has been around for a long time. It was based on the concept of creating and maintaining a Christian nation by ensuring a close relationship of power between Church authority and the State.[127] This came at a price; by gaining access to the seats of power, the church gave up much of its original independence as a distinct group of people with a particular communal vision and mission. This created a mindset based on a power discourse;[128] whereby 'Christendom' describes a 'church-state' relationship typified by:

- Creation of a hierarchical church society and the loss of lay vitality.
- Power-hierarchy created an institution rather than a community.
- Orientation towards maintaining the status quo. As church moved from the margins to the centre of society.
- Wanting to control history and bring in God's Kingdom through political power. Compelled all to be 'Christian' with resultant loss

of true mission.

- Assuming Christians would govern nations more justly and effectively than others or that having Christians in influential positions would be beneficial.
- A punitive rather than restorative approach to justice.
- An interpretation of Church history that marginalises the laity, dissident movements, women and the poor.
- Forms of Church that disempower the laity from active participation in leadership and liturgy.
- Inattentiveness of the criticisms of those outraged by the historic association of Christianity with patriarchy, warfare, injustice and patronage.
- Partiality for respectability, top-down mission and hierarchical church government.
- Approaches to evangelism that rely excessively on 'come' rather than 'go' initiatives.
- Thinking that the Christian story is still known, understood and widely believed within society.
- Preoccupation with the rich and powerful.
- Consider churchgoing a normal social activity and that most people should feel comfortable in church buildings and services.
- Privatisation and individualisation of faith.

Arguably this mindset is anachronistic to many people living in contemporary postmodern culture.[129] In other words, the rise of the postmodern epoch requires a shift in the relationship between church and state, as described by 'Christendom'. Indeed, the term 'post-Christendom' has already been coined (and in fact widely used) to describe just a shift.[130] Murray defines a 'post-Christendom' new Church-State relationship as:[131]

- Renouncing imperialistic approaches to language and cultural imposition, making 'truth claims' with humility and respecting other view points.
- Holistic forms of faith – that seek to integrate the public private split.
- To move from the centre to the margins of the relationship between Church and State.

- From privileged place in society to a voice amongst others in pluralism.
- From control to witness.
- From maintenance to mission.
- From institution to movement.

This post-Christendom mindset has a lot to do with the way that the church operates as a spiritual community. Holding this mindset resonates with 'postmodern sensibilities'.

It is no co-incidence that post-Christendom is mainly the experience of Christians living in Western Europe[132], which again has a correlation with postmodernism as defined in Chapter Two. So how do these values of post-Christendom relate to the values and sensibilities of postmodernity? Sociological research completed by Jamieson identifies some of the problems associated with being a traditional or 'inherited' form of church of a modernist perspective, attempting to connect with people from a postmodern context. In his research he identified several reasons why people became 'de-churched' (that is moved outside of a regular church community) in such situations:[133]

(1) The changing societal culture that contemporary western dwellers find themselves in; specifically this time of transition between the erosion of influence of modernity and the increasing influence of postmodernity.

(2) The Structure, beliefs and faith practices of churches.

(3) The faith development of individuals located within churches and significantly influenced by societal changes brought with the transition to an increasingly postmodernist society.

The transcripts give other evidence of this:

> There are huge numbers of people who will never access the Christian faith through existing culturally alien flavours. Not to say they're not helpful for some. But more attempts are needed to engage with, listen to and understand the missing cultures ... the numbers leaving tell us the current way of doing things is being rejected. [134]

It is a cultural shift, the traditional church doesn't reflect the culture and that's why our people are not relating to the church, they are just turning off.[135]

I began to see that although it was attracting non-church people who wouldn't normally come to church it was still too big a gap for them who showed interest to say 'now we need to go to a normal church' and so I began to think actually we needed to create a different type of community.[136]

Well you see I had given up on church … for various reasons, just been hurt by church, that's it, me and church are over. Me and God, fine, but as far as church is concerned, that was it ….[137]

People wanted and needed a spiritual nourishment that they weren't finding elsewhere.[138]

I started the church because for personal reasons I wanted there to be a church that my friends could go to … who most of which were in their 20s and 30s mostly non-church going … it was a great divide in my life between my church and the world I lived in … I wanted to bridge the gap between them.[139]

So the answer to the question – "Can traditional churches adapt to meet these changing needs of new ways of relating and communicating with-and-to more postmodern aspects of contemporary society?" appears to be 'no', if the content of the transcripts is significant. Clearly Jamieson, Cray, Riddell, Warren and others hold this position, that 'inherited' and traditional forms of church cannot – alone - meet this postmodern need because they operate within particular (premodern and modern) contexts. So the challenge to 'Fresh Expressions' then is to model ways of being church that make significant connection with the more postmodern aspects of our current culture. We will now explore aspects of postmodern contemporary culture that can be utilised by 'Fresh Expressions' as points of connection.

Hunger for relationship & belonging today

Many have noted as a starting place for 'Fresh Expressions' the 'turn-to-relationship' in our culture, driven by consumption, which has led to a renewed appreciation of forms of church as community. Grenz, Warren and Greenwood put this well:[140]

One of the most crucial hallmarks of the postmodern situation is what might be termed the "turn to relationships." ... humans are fundamentally social creatures and therefore the emptiness individuals sense can never be filled by the abundance of possessions but only in relationships with others.

The breakdown of many social relationships has left people with a hunger for relationships, for some sense of belonging ... far more on the basis of network (fluid, light-structured, democratic, motivational groups) ....[141]

Our world is calling out for social structures that will be more fluid and flexible, more open-ended and mobile, more creative and adventuresome, less self-reliant and more interdependent in their basic orientation.[142]

A number of comments in the transcripts support this desire for a new form of church-as-community:

We have grown organically [as church] through friendships. Really the word friendship underlies everything that we do.[143]

These forms of community are not neat and tidy and are somewhat chaotic, as A Etzioni, 1998 stated:

People are members of several communities simultaneously ... community boundaries are fluid, overlapping, and even intertwined.[144]

In a culture where people are constantly searching for a sense of identity and belonging, the function of church as a spiritual community becomes an important focus for mission:

The communities' constitutive narrative provides a transcendent vantage point for life in the here and now. It bestows a qualitative meaning upon time and space, and upon the community members as they inhabit their world .... The Church is more than an aggregate of all its members, for it is a particular people imbued with a particular "constitutive narrative" ....[145]

This thinking resonates with a creative understanding of church as community:

At the heart of a post-modern Christian ecclesiology is the concept of the church as community. More specifically the Christian church is a particular community marked by certain characteristics.[146]

A missionary church is relational ... it is characterised by welcome and hospitality. Its echoes and style are open to change when new members join.[147]

The transcripts give evidence of being this type of fluid-church-as-community.

[Our] church is like an open source computer platform of the gospel rather than a Microsoft product. By that I mean, what we do, as church together, we take the source code as the gospel but around that code, everyone has a particular part to play, equally in making this 'kingdom-system' work ... Everyone contributes ... offering their gifts, and every time a new person comes into the community the DNA changes, it never stays the same, it's not static, it's not issued in a box-version 2.0.[148]

It is hard for traditional forms of church to take the significant risks to meet these emerging social forms. The Church needs 'Fresh Expressions' to enable such innovation and experimentation, but always by working in collaboration in a mixed economy, where the traditional continues to relate to the premodern and modern aspects of culture. This requires a process as Brown has stated:

To attempt to incorporate some social groupings into the Church as it is would be to attempt too many steps at once. First, the new social groupings ... needs to find its theological, liturgical and ecclesial voice

... Like all innovative ventures, there is uncertainty about whether they are about modelling a future norm or filling a present and future niche. In other words the 'Orange Effect' ('the future is bright the future is orange') or the 'Heineken effect' ('refreshes the parts other churches don't reach') that we are anticipating when we open the way to new mission initiatives. The proper answer will start with the 'Heineken effect' ....[149]

In this way, 'Fresh Expressions' are concerned with 'being' church rather than 'going' to church to engage with a postmodern context. Many seeking to 'refresh the parts other churches cannot reach'.

The emerging churches seek to answer the question what it means to "be" church rather than "go" to church ....[150]

Firstly then as we have already established, there is a hunger for relationship today, where creative and fluid forms of community modelled by fresh expressions of church seek to connect.[151] What other points of connection are there between 'Fresh Expressions' of church and postmodern culture?

New forms of spirituality

Another fascinating phenomena associated with postmodernity is the renewed spiritual exploration for personal meaning. This often presents itself as more of a searching 'pick and mix' approach to spirituality borne out of people who define their lives by patterns of consumption.[152] Much of this searching is created by the rejection of an inherited story with few distinguishing fixed points. Such an approach to defining the self creates an existential angst as it does not seek to engage with the major questions of life. So people have to constantly reinvent themselves, and life becomes a pattern of embedding, disembedding and re-embedding.[153] People are searching for an authenticating narrative that gives meaning to themselves, the planet and the universe. Additionally Rollins, Caputo and Davis have attributed increased spirituality directly to the development of communication and information technologies in contemporary culture. They argue that information technology itself has created a new spiritual belief in the impossible:

The impossible has recently become possible again, that the very force of modernist criticism when turned on itself opens the way for a post-critical and post-secular posture that accommodates the passion for the impossible. That movement of living on the limit of the possible, in hope for expectation of the impossible, a reality beyond the real, which I take to be the mark of a religious sensibility ... We live ... in a world of high-tech advanced telecommunication systems, a dizzying world that is changing everything ... Religion shows every sign of ... flourishing in a new high-tech form.[154]

Cell phones whose signals easily penetrate thick walls, satellites that link across the globe ... we have found a way to mime the angels.[155]

We are faced with an amazing – shall we say an impossible? – situation: the simultaneous flourishing of science and religion, and indeed, at its extremes, of advanced hardball science along with some far out screwball superstition. We live in a world where the most sophisticated scientific and high-tech achievements cohabit ... Fundamentalists, New-Age spiritualities, and belief in all sorts of bizarre hocus-pocus phenomena ... However there is increasing rejection of traditional forms of spirituality.[156]

This form of 'hyper-real'[157] faith, makes connections with pre-modern forms of mysticism reframed into a new postmodern context:

So here we are: a hypertechnological and cynically postmodern culture seemingly drawn like a passel of moths toward the glittering flames of the premodern mind.[158]

Today's techgnotics find themselves, consciously or not, surrounded by a complex set of ideas and images: transcendence through technology ....[159]

Arguably it is no co-incidence that communication and visual technologies are employed in experimental forms of worship, which enchant and create a sense of awe and use images that connect with contemporary culture.

This idea of proclaiming afresh in each generation the gospel ... I think using a data projector with Apple Mac lap tops is on a surface level, very new to some people who come to our services, but on a deeper level, I think that nothing we do is new at all. It's drawing on the tradition, but packaged in a contemporary way.[160]

I had passing conversations with people on [internet] chat rooms and things, and they have said you are lucky to belong to such a spiritual community, eventually as a result of these cyber connections, they have gone along and checked out our website....[161]

This form of 'impossible' mystical spirituality is not all good news. As was stated in the last chapter, the process of globalisation itself can create forms of fundamentalism. Further, belief in the 'impossible' also can create in Caputo's words the 'impossible people', in that forms of fundamentalist faith and church practice can easily take root in this form of spiritual environment, that can become oppressive, controlling and violent.[162] Fresh Expressions of church then could have a key role in countering these more unhealthy forms of Christianity, in living out contextual forms of faith and church that do not seek to oppress, control or legitimate violence.

New forms of communication, listening & dialogue

Changes in information technology and social relating give further opportunities for points of connection between Fresh Expressions and postmodern culture regarding communication. Even the way we communicate is different in postmodernity from modernity. Percy puts this well:

The relationship between words and images has changed in contemporary culture. In a post-foundational world, it is the power of the image that takes us to the text. The bible is no longer a principal source of morality, functioning as a rulebook. The gradualism of postmodernity has transformed the text into a guide, a source of spirituality, in which the power of the story as but one potential moral reference point has superseded the didactic. Thus the meaning of the Good Samaritan is more important than the Ten Commandments

– even assuming that the latter could be remembered in any detail by anyone. Into this mileau the image speaks with power.[163]

Fresh Expressions are in a good position to listen, engage and dialogue with postmodern culture, through creative approaches to communication.[164]

> We have being running one [event] on 'risk and fear' … It is going to be different in that it's going to be a fusion between a sort of art and creative worship service with art installations around so that people can view those as [a form of] presentation … with story telling and interviews in a warehouse … as a shop window event.[165]

Engaging & reframing consumption

As Baker has said, the key point of connection for 'Fresh Expressions' of church centres on relating to a postmodern culture that is based on consumption.

> The single most important challenge the church faces in the Western world is how to relate the Christian faith to a culture that runs under the logic of consumption … An approach based on persuading people of the truth of Christianity's claims is no longer answering the questions that are asked. In a culture swamped with advertising, we've had enough of sales pitches. Those who claim to know all the answers are viewed with suspicion … The church should reshape practice.[166]

'Fresh Expressions' need to provide navigable space for people who are postmodern tourists, seeking to consume spiritual experience: space for development and discipleship through tour guides and resources – 'spirituality to go'.[167]

> My friends in Chicago, they started out meeting together in a pub because there was a food international dinner night and that's how we all got … together and ate and talked about life and God, about spirituality always over food and drink included.[168]

> [At] our Living Room [Café Church] … people come and make community happen with us here … An open store experience, there is no

scheduling for the Living Room, what people bring is what happens here so if somebody walks in and says I am an artist I say great if you would like to show your art here, or I am a musician I want to do a Jazz show, so we have a Jazz show ….[169]

There are people we have been in contact with … they find their way to us through our website or through friends. We actually give out to a bigger scene probably than we were expecting.[170]

Importantly, there is also some evidence in the transcripts that groups enable people to shift from being consumers to producers:

We are … shifting from being … consumers of church to producers of contextual forms of Church.[171]

So by providing forms of church that engage with consumption and provide real community, such forms of church provide opportunities for people to explore and belong, and shift from being spiritual consumers to spiritual producers. This enables people to get beyond the limitations of purely consumptive behaviour that seeks to 'take' counter-culturally enabling people to start 'giving'. In so doing, 'real-community-as-church' happens.

Enthusiasm for trying out new ways of doing things

Within postmodern culture, Warren also identifies a renewed hunger for a sense of experimentation and risk taking. People are keen to innovate. 'Fresh Expressions' can respond to this call for church to be a pilot project (missionary in nature) of the new humanity established by Christ.[172]

I would argue that mission is part of the kind of DNA of what we are about … we have done for a couple of years the 'mind body and spirit' fair which is a New Age Fair at Manchester … To have your taro read … you can buy the essence of 'Christ' which is a perfume spray, this is essentially a commercial sense spirituality, and so within that context we provided a kind of sacred space, a place for people to pray. In the space there were different spiritual installations … people could wash their hands, use a plasma ball, drop a stone, join in a prayer wall and on top of that we offered prayer for healing and just prayed with people … People were just really pleased to see us there. I think they got a certain amount of security from it, seeing a Christian Church in that context.[173]

Renewed interest in the ancient reframed in the contemporary.

As identified earlier in this chapter, there is (with postmodern culture) a return to a form of mysticism and belief in the impossible. This form of spirituality is a re-framing of something premodern. Some writers have written about 'Fresh Expressions' drawing on the experiences of the Mystics as a place of spiritual resource in times of change.

> The work of Michel de Certeau explored how the mystics in the 17th century reconfiguring faith so that it becomes vital and life giving. He began to see the edges of church and culture as opportunities rather than crisis. He began to see that those who surf the edges as creative and vital renewers of faith. In times of cultural fragmentation, he observed, new and creative life emerged on the edges. He observed numerous transformative processes. Change in culture did not drip down from above but happened through experimentation from below or rather at the edges holding onto cultural memories and hopes. Old resources in new situations …. [174]

A number of the study projects articulated this sense of 'mystical reframing' through an 'ancient-future' approach.[175] The transcripts, web and blog sites give evidence of exploring the 'ancient-mystical' reframed into the current. Examples include labyrinths, Celtic body prayers, mystical forms of meditation, explorations of the spirituality of films, story-telling and forms of contemplation.[176] In this way, Fresh Expressions reframe two millennia of resources for use in the present.

Postmodern return to a more feminine understanding of God and the church

Some have associated cultural change with the concept of 'birthing', and the need to assimilate a more nurturing approach towards people and cultural values.[177] It is essential that this also reflects power structures, for example, flat forms of leadership modelled on empowerment. Gladwin has summarised this as follows:

The emerging church will have four features in common:

1. Focus on the journey of faith and the experience of God;
2. Desire for less structure and more direct involvement by participants;
3. Sense of flexibility in order and a distinctly non-hierarchical culture;
4. Recognition that the experience of church is about the sustaining of discipleship.

So the church will focus on core faith, on minimum essential order, on people and their gifts, on flexible patterns of life held together in communion and on a shared sense of community.[178]

This study's four Fresh Expressions projects resonate with these more nurturing values, as is constantly articulated through the transcripts.[179]

Recreating public space

In more 'modernist' contexts, some have written about the erosion of shared living space in our cities and neighbourhoods, with an increased focus on the privatisation of space. The opportunities for social interaction in shared space have diminished to consumptive moments such as getting a taxi or paying for something in a shop.[180] In postmodernism, there is an increased sensibility of providing opportunities for interaction and relationship. Urban regeneration is an example of the values of promoting the revival of public shared space. 'Fresh Expressions' of church have a contribution to make to ensure that they are truly incarnational in mission –'go to them'.

At bottom, religion, like the public life, has to do with unity, with the overcoming of brokenness and fragmentation, with the reconciliation of that which has been estranged. The very root of the word religion means to 'rebind' or 'bind together,' ... For the church preaches a vision of human unity ... If so, then the church must incarnate its vision in public.[181]

Café churches, and 'social projects that have become churches' are examples of church-as-public-space initiatives. So not only can Fresh Expression of church relate to consumption and other postmodern sensibilities, they can also respond to the increased need for forms of church that engage and legitimise real public space.

All the study projects identified a sense of engaging with public space; Sanctus 1 with the city centre of Manchester, B1 with the city centre of Birmingham; COTA with the Fremont area of Seattle; and Moot in Westminster, London.[182] All use various creative activities aiming to build a presence with these areas, in interaction with strangers.

To conclude, we have established that the church from its creation has constantly reformed throughout history in response to changes in culture. Statistics and statistical predictions suggest that traditional and inherited forms of church will be unable to meet the gap between church and the postmodern elements of contemporary culture. Therefore Fresh Expressions are needed to meet these perceived gaps. An exploration of the effect of the 'Christendom' mindset gives additional evidence that traditional and inherited forms of church find it difficult to hold values resonant with postmodernism. Rather, postmodernism requires a 'post-Christendom' mindset, for genuine engagement between Church and the emerging culture.

Finally, the possibilities for 'Fresh Expression' mission, coming out of postmodern sensibilities were explored drawing on examples from the transcripts that include: hunger for relationship and belonging as 'church as community'; new forms of spirituality and how 'fresh expressions' can engage with this; new forms of communicating, listening and dialogue through events, experience and the arts; engaging and reframing consumption; enthusiasm for trying out new ways of doing things; renewed interest in the ancient reframed into the contemporary; the need for church to adopt a more nurturing approach to social change; and the renewal of public space and the need for the church to be present with the stranger.

It is the authors' contention, that these opportunities arising out of the postmodern elements of contemporary culture enable 'Fresh Expressions' of church to engage with forms of mission and 'being church' in ways that traditional and inherited forms of church cannot.

Chapter Four

What makes these new forms church?

This chapter will explore how the four study projects are being authentic forms of church. This task is not straightforward, as there is no universally accepted definition or doctrine. However, there is much writing on the various approaches to understanding the ecclesiological and functional significance of 'church'. Analysis of the transcripts indicates that there are six significant themed groupings of how the studies' contributors understand the ecclesiology and function of their projects as 'being church'. These themes will be explored as possible evidence of authentic ecclesiology using Dulles' 'Models of church', the 'credal marks of the church', and (importantly) the 'Marks of the Missional church'.

Church as the reflection of the character of the Trinitarian God

The most common reference in the transcripts to an understanding of the meaning of church was in connection to the Holy Trinity. Specifically, that the church as a spiritual community should reflect the mystical Holy community of the Godhead.

> Our starting point was community. On our first flyer we used the words Christian community. Regarding worship, mission and community, community as with the Trinity was the starting point … developing that sense of community reflects what is happening in the Trinity ….[183]

Additionally, it was apparent, that the famous Rublev's Icon "The Trinity" was an important image that expressed this understanding for many of the groups.[184] As an image, it has been blended into both group web and blog sites, and as a visual it is commonly used within forms of worship. In the interviews, this icon was often present in many of the homes, gatherings, and offices visited. This icon and what it expresses clearly brings a wealth of meaning to the groups concerning the nature of God and how this relates to being Church.

> The words Holy Spirit, Incarnation, the Godhead trinity as community, we always take that extremely seriously … If you want to get even deeper in this whole place it is basically our way of putting ourselves into the Rublev's icon of the whole church – it models what we as community should be to reflect the Godhead.[185]

I know that a number of people identify quite happily with Rublev's icon as church being a place of embrace, welcoming, as participation, all those resonances that you have with the idea of Trinitarian theology, ideas encapsulated in that would resonate with the group.[186]

Clearly the concept of the Church modelled on the nature of the Trinity, (or what is called the 'periochoresis')[187] articulates the shared values and function of church for the study projects. This resonates strongly with postmodern forms of ecclesiology:

> Ultimately then, we enjoy the fullness of community as, and only as God graciously brings us to participate together in the fountainhead of community, namely, the life of the triune God ... The community that is ours is nothing less than shared participation – a participation together – in the perichoretic community of Trinitarian persons.[188]

> In the end, participation in the perichoretic dance of the triune God as those who by the Spirit are in Christ is what constitutes community in the highest sense and hence marks the true church ....[189]

Ward argues that an understanding of Church modelled on the Trinity allows for a more fluid form of church:

> If God is seen as a flow of relationships among Father, Son, and Holy Spirit, then we find here a significant boost to a more fluid kind of church.[190]

Volf argues that this form of church as participation in the communion of the triune God, (which brings hope and present experience), has a strong New Testament basis.[191] The identity of church comes from the identity of the Trinity. The words used by Volf imply an understanding that the New Testament Church, modelled on its identity of the Trinity, was the very first form of an 'emerging church':

> New Testament authors portray the church, which emerged after Christ's resurrection and the sending of the Spirit, as the anticipation

of the eschatological gathering of the entire people of God ... The eschatological fulfilment of the high-priestly prayer of Jesus, (John 17:21) I ask ... that they may all be one. As you, Father, are in me and I am in you, may they also be in us.[192]

Furthermore, the mutual giving and receiving of such a mystical community are modelled on a Trinity that are mutually abiding and interpenetrative:

So that you may know and understand that the Father is in me and I am in the Father (John 10:38, 14:10-11, 17:21).[193]

Volf also argues, that the church reflects (in an incomplete form) the restoration of humanity back into relationship with God, as a form of eschatological hope of a God that seeks to restore the whole of creation back into right relationship with the Triune God head (1 Corinthians 12:4-6).[194]

This eschatological understanding of the Church has a strong focus on the place of the Church in the time between Pentecost (the birthing of the Church) and the consummation (the fulfilment of God's restorative vision). Therefore, it relates strongly to Brown's understanding of a 'theology of the interim'[195] or in the 'now but not yet' Kingdom. Furthermore, there appears to be a connection between this mystical understanding of the Church reflecting the Trinity and the function of mission - to seek to make disciples - an incarnational vision of catching up with what God is doing in the world and culture. In other words a view that the God of relationship seeks to restore people into discipleship and right relationship with the Divine, and this is 'mission', (2 Corinthians 4). For example, one project used Tarot cards to convey the meaning of the Trinity at a 'New Age Fair', as a mission event:

When discussing the Trinity ... we were talking about [using] Tarot and if you look at the symbols buried in icons in the same way that you look at symbols buried in Tarot, you can see that there are resonances of all sorts of stuff, hidden meanings, disguised things which need to be brought to life ... it is really nice to sit in church and look at an icon, [but] when you go out of church you are not going to continue carrying an icon round to people saying 'hey look it has two fingers on the table that means …' they don't get it, but you can find other ways of doing that in the real world.[196]

The relationship with the Divine therefore becomes fluid and dynamic, a form of transcendent event and encounter, knowing God through experience rather than knowing God through propositional facts. This is a dynamic form of missionary encounter:

> Any attempt to image God contextually is in fact an act of God reading us. As we embody God, as we proclaim God in community, God looks back, questioning the church: Is the church fully representing the image of God? Is the church a participatory place where people find their full humanity in Christ? Is the body of God a true ikon of God? …"Will we let the image of God construct us? [197]

This idea of the church as a missionary event is not just a Catholic idea, but draws on Evangelical theologians too, for example Yoder:

> The Church was … not merely the agency or the constituency of a mission programme, the contents of which were essentially distinct from its practices and institutions. The community was the mission.[198]

The understanding of church as the reflection of the perichoresis correlates to Dulles' work on 'models of church'. In this, Dulles promotes a typology of five major understandings of church, the second of which she calls 'The Church as Mystical Communion'.[199] It is the author's contention that the form of postmodern ecclesiology expressed in the transcripts corresponds to this second model.

Dulles' typology of 'The Church as Mystical Communion' is summarised as:[200]
- Not an institution but a fraternity.
- Church as interpersonal community.
- The 'I thou' is no longer essentially a demanding, but a giving one.
- Church as a fellowship of persons – a fellowship of people with God and with one another in Christ.
- Connects strongly with the mystical 'body of Christ' as a communion

of the spiritual life of faith, hope and charity.

- Resonates with Aquinas' notion of the Church as the principle of unity that dwells in Christ and in us, binding us together and in him.

- All the external means of grace, (sacraments, scripture, laws etc) are secondary and subordinate; their role is simply to dispose people for an interior union with God effected by grace.

The concept of the 'body of Christ' is an important element of this understanding of Church.[201]

Dulles sees this form of church as empowering its members to fully participate in the life of the spiritual community, animated by supernatural faith and charity, as the Church seeks to lead people into communion with the Divine.[202] Because of its fluidity, Dulles believes that this form of church is good at adapting and responding to social change.[203] Regarding churchmanship, Dulles sees the strength in this approach as being acceptable to both Protestant and Catholic:

> In stressing the continual mercy of God and the continual need of the Church for repentance, the model picks up themes of Protestant theology ... [and] in Roman Catholicism ... when it speaks of the church as both holy and sinful, as needing repentance and reform ...

> The biblical notion of Koinona, ... that God has fashioned for himself a people by freely communicating his Spirit and his gifts ... this is congenial to most Protestants and Orthodox ... [and] has an excellent foundation in the Catholic tradition.[204]

It is therefore unsurprising that this framework enables Church to reflect the 'both-and' vision of the Emerging Church, drawing on the best of the Catholic and Evangelical traditions explored in Chapter One, and that it is an expression of mystical faith that reflects the forms of relational and mystical spirituality arising out of the postmodern elements of our culture explored in Chapters Two and Three. In this way, this study's projects also reflect three of the five stated values of the 'Missionary Church' as stated in the Mission-Shaped Church report:[205]

- A missionary church is focused on God the Trinity. Worship lies at the heart of a missionary church, and to love and know God as Father, Son and Spirit is its chief inspiration and primary purpose ....

- A missionary church is incarnational ... [it] seeks to shape itself in relation to the culture in which it is located or to which it is called ....

- A missionary church is relational ... [it] is characterised by welcome and hospitality. Its echoes and style are open to change when new members join ....

However, as Dulles articulates, there are some shortcomings to this way of 'being Church':[206]

- So biological that it is difficult to define the Church.
- Danger of over spiritualising and deifying the activity of the Church. If the Holy Spirit were conceived as the life principle of the Church, all actions of the Church would seem to be attributed to the Holy Spirit, which can obscure the personal responsibility and freedom of the members. In such situations there could be issues relating to power and unhealthy forms of community.
- The significance of the incarnation (humanness) of Christ is reduced.[207]
- Danger of seeing your form of church as the only legitimate form of contextual church, loss of the sense of the wider picture of the church catholic.
- Whilst the Church promises communion, it does not always provide it in very evident forms. Christians commonly experience the Church more as a companionship of fellow travellers on the same journey than as a union of lovers dwelling in the same house.
- The organisational and hierarchical aspects of the church are neglected and appear superfluous.

These are very real issues; that raise legitimate questions for this study's projects, which will be addressed in the next chapter. However in general, the 'emerging church' subset of Fresh Expressions of Church does appear to legitimately correlate with the typology of 'Church as Mystical Communion'.

Church as Body of Christ, Ekklesia & Transformative Community

The second most significantly stated grouping, relates to the concepts of the Body of Christ and Ekklesia, as well as the function of Church and its members to transform society. As has already been stated, there is a relationship between the biblical term 'body of Christ' and the Church as 'Mystical Communion'.

> For me, it is the whole picture of rootedness ... the importance of the rootedness of church if it is going to sustain real relationships. To be a 'body of Christ'.[208]

> Church indicates the succession ... of an ongoing tradition ... a sense of the body of Christ on earth ... we are part of a much broader thing in the spiritual sense ....[209]

The 'body of Christ' is the dominant image in the Apostle Paul's theology of church reflected in 1 Corinthians chapter 10 and 12, and in Colossians and Ephesians. To be 'in Christ' is to be 'made anew', to be re-created. Paul's vision was not specifically about geographical unity, but more of a common allegiance or connection to Christ.[210] Such an understanding would include a more network-focused culture, such as we are now experiencing. In Romans and 1 Corinthians the image connects diversity with unity. Our connection to Christ makes us part of the body. In this way, the church emerges out of the activity of everyone who is joined in Christ. For people to understand the significance of Christ, to consider such a relational connection requires articulation of the significance of Christ and of the Kingdom of God, hopefully 'lived-out' by church. Traditionally this is understood as teaching, evangelism, baptising and nurturing new believers. In the context of the case study projects, this is understood as belonging without necessarily believing, experiencing Christ through interaction with the spiritual community, and hearing the stories about God, which hopefully become their story:

> We have grown organically through ... friendship evangelism as giving a taster ... many people experience ... our events and stay.[211]

> [It is about] a public arena, a coffee shop, to allow people to come and to sit and to chill and to engage in Christian spirituality.[212]

The concept of the 'body of Christ' as used by Paul also connects with his use of the concept 'Ekklesia', a New Testament word more commonly used for the 'church' as a 'gathering or assembly of people'.[213] This term is also understood to reflect the idea of living out an alternative community, one which seeks to embody the values of the 'now but not fully yet' Kingdom of God.[214] A community that does not seek to remove itself from the world, but one that seeks to transform as Christ brought transformation through his ministry by the community of the disciples.[215]

> [The Church] as the new social organism, springing from the work of Jesus in calling the twelve, with a citizen body which scandalously included from the beginning slaves, women and even children, persons who had no place in the traditional ecclesia ... obeyed his [Jesus'] new commandment to love irrespective of blood ties or social class.[216]

In the early Church, some theologians have argued that the original 'Ekklesia' was a form of 'town council' or 'local legislator' in the Greek speaking parts of the Roman Empire.[217] These assemblies were ruled by the male wealthy elite. The Christian Church as an alternative-Ekklesia, therefore, sought to live out this call to transformation through being an alternative assembly of the powerless that included slaves, the poor and women.[218] Its activities in living out the Kingdom in the now-but-not-yet were social, economic and political as well as spiritual.[219] As a consequence, the excluded are 're-membered' into the Church as an expression of the Kingdom.[220]

> Christianity entered history as a new social order ... From the very beginning Christianity was not primarily a "doctrine", but ... a "community" ... a New Community, distinct and peculiar ... to which members were called and recruited ... Primitive Christians felt themselves to be closely knit together ... in a unity which radically transcended all human boundaries – of race, of culture, of social rank, and indeed the whole dimension of "this world". [221]

Although not stated directly, some of the transcript comments correlate with this idea of a transformative ekklesia.

It is about how Jesus was with his disciples, the way he loved them, and how they belonged for three hard years before he died. What is important to me ... is how we reflect that in loving people, allowing them to belong, and encourage them to grow spiritually.[222]

Our fourth one [value] is liberation theology, community which is about justice and restorative justice ... social action ....[223]

This concept of 're-membering' also makes connection with a sacramental understanding of the significance of the Ekklesia: that at the Last Supper, Jesus re-membered the new Ekklesia through the inauguration of Eucharist or Holy Communion.[224]

The re-membering that Jesus commanded us to undertake was more profound than simply remembering past events. We are called to nothing less than a re-membering of Christ's body on earth having understood that everything in heaven and on earth should find their head and centre in the Word made flesh. In this way we are called into participation ... in the round dance of the Trinity, the perichoresis.[225]

Church as sacramental & eschatological community

The notion of Church as Mystical Communion, drawing on the concept of the Body of Christ as the transformative re-membering of the Ekklesia, has further sacramental implications and was the third most commonly expressed understanding of Church in the transcripts. As stated, this form of transcendent understanding of God interacting with people through mystical communion, extends to the whole of creation:

Emerging churches tend to have rediscovered a more sacramental approach to everyday life ... we gather around weekly Eucharist ... We try to take a sacramental view of the whole of creation ... A sacramental life is life lived in God, so each day is sacramental and we ourselves are sacraments of God in the world ... A defining characteristic of church has to be the regular participation in the community in Eucharist.[226]

This leads to another of Dulles' models, 'The Church as Sacrament'. In this typology, the church becomes an event of grace as the lives of its members are transformed in hope, in joy, in self-forgetful love, in peace, in patience, and in other Christ-like virtues.[227] A sacrament is a sign of grace, of God's gift. It is socially constituted, a communal symbol of grace coming to fulfilment.[228]

Although Dulles makes a distinction between the two models 'Church as sacrament' and 'Church as Mystical Communion', the two are very closely related. In Rublev's icon, the Trinity sits round the chalice, emphasising the Eucharist as a sacramental connection between the viewer of the icon and the Godhead.[229] In reality, the emerging church projects of this study are probably a fusion of the two Dulles' models.

The main advantage of this second model is that sacrament becomes a visible sign of the presence of the revealed God, so that spectators may encounter God or sense the significance of the Church as a numinous sign.

This has profound implications for mission. That God is made present in missionary activity by the presence of members of the church community interacting with people in the world. It is clear that some of this study's respondents are aware of this significance:

> A gift of the emerging church is that we see God equally in the Eucharist and in drinking beer together in the local bar.[230]

So reflecting back on the values of the 'Missionary Church' articulated in the 'Mission Shaped Church' report, the exploration of Ekklesia, transformation and sacrament also appear to connect with the last two of the five values:

- A missionary church is transformational ... [it] exists for the transformation of the community that it serves, through the power of the gospel and the Holy Spirit ....
- A missionary church makes disciples ... [it] is active in calling people to faith in Jesus Christ ... it encourages the gifting and vocation of all the people of God ....[231]

Church reflecting Credal Marks

Many theologians have commented on the content of the ancient Nicene Creed to help articulate the role of Church:

To describe the Church as 'one, catholic, and apostolic' is to enunciate its vocation and to remind it of its aspiration.[232]

Although the respondents do not comment greatly on this, there is an awareness of its importance.

> Fresh expressions of the one, holy, catholic and apostolic church, so [it's the] same, but fresh![233]

So how do the study's projects reflect the four identified credal marks?

The Church is One

Unity in the Church mattered to Jesus. 'Being one' was an aspiration and intention, and a goal which we are called to seek (John 17:22). This unity is not about conformity, but about unity in diversity: those of the church can disagree about a number of issues, but at the same time be able to transcend this. God is made present through the church as a 'body of Christ' even when some parts are very different from others. As Brown states:

> Unity is a mark of the Kingdom fulfilled – a central element of our eschatological hope.[234]

So what evidence is there for the importance of this idea of unity in diversity in the study groups?

> Every church is a community of the resurrection. We anticipate our eternal home, we remember our debt to Christ.[235]

> One of the ways we express this appreciation of the wider church, is through supporting mission-type work in Afghanistan, so we do I think have a vision for this wider thing. We have an active connection with other churches in Birmingham, so we do appreciate being part of a wider scene.[236]

> I think church indicates the succession from one point to another and being part of an ongoing tradition.[237]

I see us [Moot] as a congregation and part of the global church.[238]

The Church is Holy

Holiness, is a call to a distinctive and authentic expression of the Christian faith, drawing on scripture and tradition.[239] In the transcripts the concept of an 'ancient-future' faith is often mentioned. This appears to resonate with the idea of 'holiness', that Fresh Expressions seek to be faithful and true to the ecumenical creeds but reframed around the context of 'being Christian' within current, postmodern, contemporary culture:

> What comes from an ancient wisdom into a contemporary tree and there are lots of traditions ... we have talked about the desert fathers for instance which was really interesting. There are things that can be distilled or reused from that ancient wisdom into our contemporary lives.[240]

> I think it is also to do with trying to do contextual theology whilst holding onto the ancient traditions of the faith (i.e. the sacraments).[241] ... the 'ancient future' aspect of being church and doing mission.[242]

In this way, holiness is not about retreating from the world to encapsulate a more pure form of the faith, but a form of Christianity that sees Church engage with the heart of contemporary culture.

The Church is catholic

Within the wider church, the sense of being 'catholic' is about acknowledging and accepting 'diversity' as the church responds to different contexts.[243] No one local church represents the fullness of what it means to be church. This essence of church is acknowledged in the transcripts:

> I do feel the sense of a wider church community outside of B1, although the way we express it is slightly different. I am aware that many in our church community come from very different traditions so the way we experience communion is at the end quite different.[244]

The Church is Apostolic

There are two strands of meaning to this concept. The first is the idea that the church relates to the first Apostles, the disciples of Christ, which has been handed down by successive generations of Christians and Church.[245] This concept also includes the contribution of those commissioned for the role of leadership.

As was explored in the model of 'Church as Mystical Communion', there is a tension between hierarchical structures and the concept of the 'body of Christ'. However, drawing on the values we have explored in the transcripts so far, there is evidence that the groups do identify with the historic church.[246] However, the issue of Apostolic forms of leadership is one that requires more exploration.[247]

The second strand of meaning pertains to the idea of 'being sent', the idea of being commissioned for service. In a number of the transcripts, there was the sense of 'being sent' by a 'mother church' birthing a new activity such as B1[248], or by the Diocese with COTA, Moot and Sanctus 1.[249] These Fresh Expressions ministries may not have been instigated or created by Church authorities, but they have been supported and validated through the commissioning of leaders and connection to the structures of the various Dioceses.

Other New Testament words for Church

The only other metaphor not discussed so far, but raised in the transcripts, is the concept of the 'priesthood of all believers'. Again, although it is not mentioned directly, it is implied in some of the transcripts: that the Church as mystical communion of the body of Christ, the Ekklesia which has a sacramental relationship with the world, is also a community of those who are called to a shared priestly life. That all believers are Priests, drawing on the metaphor described in St Paul's Letters.

> We experience him through the Spirit … Our Church is about being those who are related and interdependent because of the symbols of the Eucharist and we would not be together if it wasn't for that.[250]

> Sanctus, it is that giving and receiving thing … participation is not just about sitting in a service and saying a prayer, its about taking part

in the community.[251]

> Church should be bottom up and instead of top down ... It's more
> about people ... having gifts and stories to share ....[252]

This further creates an understanding of 'shared leadership'. The laity and the ordained
are together the expression of the priesthood of all believers. People have different roles
of function, but there should be no hierarchy, particularly of worldly power. This idea of
shared leadership is present in the transcripts.

> Usually I work with two or three other people ... who will head that up,
> and that encourages participation because people feel there is someone
> who knows a bit more about what they are doing and so people feel a
> bit freer [to co-lead].[253]

From the evidence discussed so far, the projects appear to meet part of the fifth value of
the 'missionary church' as identified in the Mission-Shaped church report:[254]

> A missionary church makes disciples ... [it] is active in calling people
> to faith in Jesus Christ ... it encourages the gifting and vocation of all
> the people of God ....

Functional understanding of the Church

Warren crystallised his understanding of the activity of Church as 'worship, mission and
community'. Further, he stated that a church that does not have a healthy balance of
these three activities, is living an unhealthy form of spirituality.[255]

From the transcripts, and the stories about how these forms of church emerged, it becomes
clear that they started with one or two of these activities, (often mission and worship),
from which the church as community developed. All three functions are represented in
the life of the four study projects.[256]

Challenges

As has been stated, the greatest challenge to the ecclesiology of the study's Emerging
church subset of Fresh Expressions concerns the understanding of church leadership and

structure. This was identified as a weakness of the 'Church as mystical communion' model. To emphasise this, there is only one part of the 'values of the Missionary Church' expressed in the 'Mission-Shaped Church' report that have not been addressed so far, and it concerns this same issue of leadership:

A missionary church…invests in the development of leaders.[257]

There is little evidence in the transcripts for an articulation of this understanding other than developing 'event' leadership. However, the author can provide anecdotal evidence that some activity is happening in the form of leadership formation, particularly in the form of the 'testing of the call to Ordination'. At the time of writing up this study, there are two people who are proceeding through the Church of England Ordination discernment process through the Moot community, and two others through a similar system in the Diocese of Olympia in Seattle through COTA.

Although not discussed in the interviews, it is clear that all the four projects have either Licensed and Ordained Clergy or a Licensed Church Army Officer, who carry leadership roles authorised by the Church and respected by the various project church communities. So there appears to be evidence of two rival systems of thinking concerning leadership. One which is non-hierarchical and driven by a model of 'shared communal leadership' and the other as a 'mixture of the hierarchical and shared-communal'. This issue will be further discussed in the next chapter.

To conclude, the transcripts appear to resonate with forms of authentic ecclesiology. The four projects have connections with two of Dulles' models of church, primarily 'the church as mystical communion' and secondarily 'the church as sacrament'. Through these models there was a strong understanding of Trinitarian theology, of the significance of the church as 'the body of Christ' and the 'ekklesia' as foundational principles of the New Testament, birthed in the primitive church and modelled on the image of the Godhead. These models had advantages and disadvantages. The main advantages included the ability to respond to social change, the ability to relate both catholic and evangelical expressions of church, and the perception of the church in worship as a form of God's presence. The main disadvantages were the difficulty of defining church, and the risk that certain expressions of the mystical significance of the church, identify church too closely with being 'God'. This latter disadvantage can result in power abuse and reduced responsibility among members of the church. The greatest difficulty with these models concerns the understanding of church structures and leadership. These last two factors are discussed in the next chapter.

Further explorations of the Credal marks of the church showed that the project groups expressed an appreciation for the need of 'One, Holy, catholic and Apostolic' church, but again there were some problems with interpreting forms of leadership. However, there was a strong identification with the 'Priesthood of all believers' in how the groups conceived of church.

Concerning functional understandings of the church, it was established that all the projects balanced the need for worship, mission and community activities to promote a healthy sense of spirituality.

Finally, comparing the transcript information with the values of the Missionary Church identified in the Mission-Shaped Church report demonstrates that the projects meet nearly all of the five stated values. Again, the exception comes in the area of leadership – specifically the development of leaders, to be discussed in the next chapter.

Overall, the evidence presented and discussed in this chapter does, arguably, support the claim that the (studied) Fresh Expressions of church are authentic and resonate with the various 'definitions', or models, of church discussed.

Chapter Five

What makes these new forms Anglican?

It is by no coincidence that many of the UK 'non-house church' experiments with contemporary 'church-missions' have connections to the Anglican Church.[258] In this chapter, there will be an initial exploration of the origins of the 'Anglicana Ecclesiana' and contemporary understandings of Richard Hooker's historic vision for the Anglican Church. This will be followed by a comparison of the transcripts with an Anglican interpretation of the Nicene Creed of 'One, Holy, Catholic and Apostolic church'. Finally I will return to the expectations stipulated in the Toyne report, to determine whether the projects included in this study meet the expectations of what is authentically 'Anglican'.

The origins of the Anglican Church

It is important, as a starting place, not to be overly romantic about the origins of Anglicanism in the formation of the Church of England that was born out of the political conflict, religious war and violence of the reformation. In 1533 in the 'Act of in restraint of appeals', the King asserted the right as Supreme Head of all matters pertaining to the realm of England to impair the power of the Papacy in domestic English affairs.[259] This was followed by the 'Act of Supremacy' in 1536 whereby the King became the only Supreme Head on earth of the church in England called the 'Anglicana Ecclesiana'.[260] This last Act of Parliament attempted to draw the various differing traditions of church into one national Church of England, catholic and protestant together with a tightly controlled liturgy. This lasted only a short time and ended in the Commonwealth period characterised by the dominance of Puritanism. In 1648 and 1662, after the Commonwealth period, Parliament re-enacted an 'Anglican Settlement', which ejected two thousand puritan clergy out of the Church, and reinstituted an Anglican Church of England.[261] Again this form of religious intolerance created significant conflict until the Act of Toleration in 1689 conceded religious pluralism. The Church of England, as the established church, then attempted to model a form of church that was both reformed and catholic, that gave room for catholic and protestant, but with a controlled prayer book and liturgical form of expression.[262]

The influence of Richard Hooker

From 1593, Richard Hooker, an early Anglican Divine and Theologian, wrote a significant amount of material on the subject 'of the Laws of Ecclesiastical Polity'. These were compiled into a series of books which were widely published and distributed. Books one to four were published in 1597, and the further eight after his death in

1648. These published writings are said to have significant influence on the Acts of Settlement that reinstituted the Church of England.[263] Hooker's writings wrestle with the problems of the time, a concept of being Church drawing on existing forms that were deeply divided and killing each other. In particular, these texts reflect the desire for these differing traditions to be held together in some form, and suggest how they could be governed.[264]

What is fascinating is the number of resonances between Hooker's vision for the Anglican Church and the vision of contemporary emerging churches (as a subgrouping of Fresh Expressions) which will now be further explored.

Firstly, we can interpret Hooker as seeking to find an ecclesiology at a time of significant cultural shift, where the pre-modern co-existed with the modern at a time known as the Reformation. Protestantism, as a reaction to a change in culture, sought legitimacy in England as an authentic interpretation of church, and Catholicism, under the pressure of intolerance, also sought survival as a legitimate expression of church also. Although our current cultural context is very different, the vision of a church with a diverse centre is central to Hooker's writings, and can provide a framework for a contemporary understanding of a 'mixed economy of church'. Hooker clearly believed in a pluralistic Church of England, where both Catholic and Protestant could co-exist.[265] Further, Hooker states a 'both and' ecclesiology rather than an 'either or' approach.[266]

> Let not the faith which ye have in our Lord Jesus Christ, be blemished
> with particularities.[267]

This 'both and' ecclesiology goes to the very heart of Anglicanism which has been described as the practice of 'dynamic tension'.[268] It is a middle way that has not been easy to maintain, and has been described by some as a 'weakness'.[269] However, it also offers a form of 'catholic-ness' that allows for diversity. This 'both and' theology strongly relates to the vision of the emerging church quoted in Chapter Two.

Significantly, Hooker articulates an understanding of the local church as 'fluid' or 'organic', in the sense that it reflects church engaging with context.[270] Some (such as Percy) have argued that this deeply resonates with our postmodern situation, concerning the body of Christ engaging with contextual culture as well as relating to the wider church.[271]

A deeply held view expressed in Hooker's writing is the essential need for participation in every expression of church. This is derived from Hooker's participative sacramental theology, which is centred on active 'participation' in the Eucharist or Holy Communion. In turn, this relates to his understanding of church as having a dynamic, incarnational and organic nature.[272] Such an understanding resonates strongly with postmodern sensibilities of communal belonging as well as the involvement of people in Fresh Expression forms of worship.

Regarding the origins of Hooker's ecclesiology, Percy has identified the doctrine of the Trinity as his model of how the church should reflect the Godhead of three mutually interdependent identities:[273] one Church seeking unity in diversity.

> Our God is one, or rather very Oneness, and mere unity ... For being
> three, and they all subsisting in the essence of one deity ....[274]

> As a man liveth joined with others in common society and belongeth
> unto the outward politic body of the Church ....[275]

In Hooker's writing there is an openness to a truly 'catholic' church that seeks to be innovative. He was against a kind of traditionalism that prevented the church adapting its practice.[276] Taking the Trinity as his starting place and drawing on a sacramental understanding of how the Church relates to culture through participation, it could be argued that Hooker saw the Church of England as a form of 'mixed economy of church' that includes 'new forms of church' that emerge out of the interplay of church and culture. [277] As Thompson has stated:

> The Anglican will see faith not so much as the foundation we start
> from but as something that emerges in the context of the life of the
> Church. It emerges not from top down, as with the Catholic organism,
> nor from the bottom up, as with the Protestant [approach], but from
> the middle out ....[278]

Some have commented on how Hooker's writings resonate with emergent qualities:

> Hooker onward, reveals greater stress in the Churches ... self-

organising, emergent qualities like koinonia or communion … each believer has potentiality, but which are only realised through belonging to the whole … the koinonia of the Church takes up every individual into a dance that transcends her and enables her to obey the emergent divine law of love. So for Anglicans worship is 'common prayer' – a communion in prayer – and the Eucharist is not primarily either a corporate sacrifice or personal memorial but Holy Communion, a real sharing in the divine life through the body of Christ … a movement of real participation in the heavenly Christ. Christ is present in his mystical or spiritual body.[279]

Finally, one of Hooker's primary concerns was that Puritan literalism would eventually lead to what we would call a fundamentalism that by its very nature would be anti-pluralistic. [280] In Hooker's own experience and memory, there would be the experience of fundamentalist forms of Puritanism and Catholicism experienced after the death of Henry VIII. Both were extreme forms of imposition that did not value the concept of unity in diversity. Violence and oppression were used to enforce a model of conformity. Hooker's polity sought to ensure plurality and prevent separatism which could again unleash further violence and dis-unity of the Church. Although different in context, this Anglican 'middle position' as an alternative to separatism and fundamentalism has much to say to our current cultural context and the very real political problems of the current Church of England. In Chapter Three, we discussed a new form of mystical spirituality as 'belief in the impossible' which creates the danger of new forms of fundamentalism and aggressive forms of faith. Anglicanism, put in its promotion of toleration and pluralism, provides a counter-voice and another way for this form of faith to be embedded into authentic church and hence discourage fundamentalism.

So reflecting back on Chapters One to Four, much of the understanding and analysis of the ecclesiological views of the study projects resonate with these contemporary interpretations of the significance of the writings of Richard Hooker, a founding father of Anglicanism.

An Anglican Understanding of One, Holy, Catholic and Apostolic Church

In addition to the exploration of this subject in Chapter Four, this study returns to the transcripts to understand how their content resonates with particularly Anglican interpretations of this creed in church practice.

'Being One'

As identified in Chapter Four, the transcripts do acknowledge the need for unity. As explored in the Hooker section, the Anglican understanding of 'unity' as 'unity in diversity' rather than in conformity, allows a sense of 'oneness' in plurality of expression. Relating this to the 39 Articles of Faith, it is clear that they will never be an Anglican systematic theology of its 'one-ness'. Moreover, the Articles are a response to specific Sixteenth Century controversies and are largely affirmations directed against specific targets that were either anti-Trinitarian or anti-pluralistic.[281] In other words, the Articles expound a diverse centre.[282]

From the transcripts it is clear that many of the projects apply this unity in diversity not only to forms of church, but also within the same particular church community:

> We have people who have slightly different theological positions surprise surprise, and different approaches to worship and shared faith so we have come to a position of really saying we will get on with each other's own positions.[283]

This has been further complicated by the number of 'de-churched' people from many different traditions who have joined (one of) the projects, and who bring with them the sensibilities of different traditions.[284]

Being Anglican & One

From the transcripts it is clear that none of the projects hold a consensus view of identifying with an Anglican identity, as articulated in this chapter so far. There appear to be two differing voices. The first is happy to identify with Anglicanism as a rich tradition that supports their project and is informed of what Anglicanism is; and the other sees Anglicanism as 'controlling', 'irrelevant' or in 'overly hierarchical' terms, and as something therefore to be avoided.[285] As is stated by the Ordained and licensed leader of B1:

> I think slowly as we get more comfortable with what we are doing,

they [the group] are getting more comfortable with 'Anglican' in terms of understanding ... I probably would be the most Anglican of the lot, I found it to be a constant home, flexible, whilst many in 'B1', they probably don't realise what it is about, about being Anglicans.[286]

There is a general concern about the more 'Christendom' forms of Church in the transcripts. This concern of an ongoing 'Christendom' mindset is also a shared concern for a number of Anglican theologians including Leech who has said:

The history of Anglicanism is itself complex and filled with ambiguity. The close links with monarchy, aristocracy and establishment, with national identity and state, are inextricable elements of dominant Anglican history, and I see them as serious obstacles to the future of Anglicanism as a coherent tradition in the modern world.[287]

However, as the Leader of B1 articulates above, there is hope that as people become increasingly embedded into the varying projects, there appears to be an increasing value placed on 'Anglican tradition' and organisation. For example, one of the dissenting voices in Moot acknowledged:

I am quite new to Anglicanism and am still trying to work out how some of these structures work. So it's a bit of a learning curve for me.[288]

Developing an Anglican identity is clearly an important matter in how this is done, but is a matter for further research that cannot be adequately covered here.

Oneness - Seeing the Diocese as the local Church

The starting place of an Anglican understanding of the 'local church' is the Diocese.[289] This draws on the ancient understanding as articulated by Ignatius a former bishop of Rome, that every expression of 'church' in each place is fully the Church, because it is also in microcosm the universal church.[290] The Diocese draws together disparate parishes and congregations in a shared identity which expresses the tensions of a pluralistic church.[291]

In the transcripts there were differing responses to this idea. All the projects at some level worked collaboratively with other local Diocesan churches of varying traditions.[292] All had some form of relationship with the Diocesan bishop and local church structures, and contributed to the financial needs of the Diocese although this was done in different ways.[293] One of the projects hosted a service for the Bishop to confirm people from varying local diocesan churches.[294] One also assisted the Diocese to construct a local children's communion policy.[295] One at Easter participated in joint traditional Anglican services in Passion Week.[296] However, at the same time, the problems with the legal pastoral measure outlined in Chapter One meant that many of the projects included in this study were not recognised as 'legitimate' churches, but at present as 'creative forms of mission' which therefore prevented members of the groups from participating in normal Diocesan and national governance structures and activities.[297] A number of the group leaders attended local Deanery meetings.[298] Some members of the groups also showed active interest in the outcomes of national and local synod meetings of the Church, as they grew in Anglican identity.[299]

Oneness – Seeing Anglicanism as a particular Communion

Anglicans share a common historical and geographical origin as a specific relationship called 'communion'. They have a 'constitution' which can be found in a whole range of history, precedent, legislation, and literature. This wide understanding of Anglicanism is expressed in the world wide Anglican Communion. There is still a common liturgy, but no longer a single Prayer Book; indigenous liturgies have replaced the original Elizabethan text. Anglicans no longer share fully interchangeable ministry because some provinces have moved ahead of others in the ordination of women, and not all parts of the Communion have as yet been able to accept their ministry. The Anglican Communion of today is more a federation of churches, some national, some regional who hold a relational-communion with the Archbishop of Canterbury, as the symbolic Head of Anglicanism.[300]

When asked about 'Anglicanism' in this wider understanding, projects in the Church of England did not articulate this other than a passing mention of the 'Archbishop of Canterbury' in one of the transcripts. Clearly this level of 'Anglicanism' is not understood or appreciated, other than the Archbishop's support and vision for 'Fresh Expressions of Church'. However, when looking at the project associated with the Episcopal Church of the United States of America, there was greater appeal to this form of 'one-ness'.[301]

Other Anglican expression of one-ness

From the transcripts, on a number of occasions, there is an appreciation of the liturgical framework and resources of the Church of England and the Episcopal Church of the United States.[302] One group explicitly articulated that they drew on the Church liturgical calendar, and also on Saints days, joining in with the wider Anglican Church in worship.[303] The importance of patterns of prayer as a basis of expression was also articulated,[304] a key element to Anglican expressions of worship drawing on the singing or saying of particular lectionary readings.

Regarding Anglican Canon law, it was again made clear that a number of the projects respected the need for consistency and lawful use of forms of Eucharist or Holy Communion.[305] Finally, two out of the four projects were official 'ecumenical partnerships' reflecting national covenants in the UK between the Church of England, and the Methodist Church in England, and in the USA, between the Episcopal Church of the United States of America, and the Evangelical Lutheran Church of the United States of America.[306] These last two projects faced the challenge of establishing an Anglican identity as well as a Lutheran or Methodist identities. This remains an important challenge for these various traditional forms of church in their development of 'Fresh Expressions' and raises another area of further research that cannot be adequately explored here.

'Being Holy': Triad/Quadrilateral – Scripture, Reason, Tradition & Experience

From the earliest days of Hooker's writing, there is a well-concerned double bind when it comes to the authority of Holy Scripture and the Church's distinctiveness in how it promotes and lives out authentic Christianity.[307] On the one hand, Hooker affirms that Scripture has a primary sacred authority; on the other, he acknowledges that Scripture cannot teach itself, as it is a matter of faith and reason.[307] Hooker initially warned against too much reliance on the "aspect of experience which has to do with feelings".[308] However, this approach was widely embraced as a distinctive Anglican Ministry as 'Scripture, Reason, Tradition', which was then expanded to include 'experience', where the first on this list ranks in importance in the process of discerning Anglican Christian ministry.[309] So as with Article 20 of the Thirty Nine articles describing the Church as 'witness and keeper'; the Bible had and has a 'controlling authority', so that, in Anglicanism, we need to submit to Scripture to draw on the grace of the truth of God which brings salvation, and to grow in 'Christlikeness', whilst still questioning its meaning in context.[310] Although, as many have said, there is a danger in simplifying this process which is by its nature very complex,[311] there is nevertheless an important attempt to establish a theology of 'correctives', to ensure that church does not become rigid and unchanging, or biblically literalist, balanced against the need to be distinctive and authentic, a divine vocation for all Anglican Churches.[312]

Although there is not much detail in the transcripts, there is evidence of an appreciation of this Anglican triad/quadrilateral, and the form of messiness that such an approach takes.

> Questioner : What makes these new forms Anglican?
>
> Group Leader 2 & 1: Being willing to stand in the broad Anglican tradition of reason, scripture and tradition ... The messiness of it, the incarnational focus.[313]

'Being Catholic'

In the context of unity in diversity, the various churches of the Anglican Communion identified key features that needed to be observed to maintain Anglican distinctiveness in what has been called the 'Chicago-Lambeth Quadrilateral of 1886/8' which stated:[314]

- The Holy Scriptures of the Old and New Testament as the revealed Word of God.
- The Nicene Creed as the sufficient statement of the Christian faith.
- The two sacraments, baptism and the Supper of the Lord, ministered with unfailing use of Christ's words of institution and of the elements ordained to him.
- The historic episcopate, locally adapted in the methods of its administration to the varying needs of the nations and peoples called of God into the unity of His Church.

Although the five transcripts did not give explicit evidence that these expectations were fully met, it is clear that through the relationships with their Diocesan Bishops, through sticking to authorised liturgies for Holy Communion and Eucharist, through activities that engaged with the Bible as Holy Scripture, and through the use of the Nicene Creed in services, that these expectations have been largely endorsed.[315]

'Being Apostolic' – The Ordinal

The Ordinal is another ancient formula found in the 'Book of Common Prayer' and more recently in the Church of England's 'Common Worship'. This document recognises the three levels of ordained ministry as 'Deacons, Priests and Bishops'.[316] The concept of the Episcopal succession of Bishops as passed down from the Apostles is a central tenet of the Anglican understanding of the Apostolic role of the Church.[317] Clearly, the projects recognise the need for this form of leadership in connection with Bishops[318], however, a number of the responses in the transcripts suggest real problems with the two other forms of ordained leadership which requires further exploration.

> Person 2: We are starting to work on … developing leadership.
> Questioner: Maybe someone within Sanctus 1 … maybe coming along and actually getting ordained?
> Person 2: … I disagree with the premise about having an ordained person.[319]

Issues with Leadership & Authority

In one of the four group transcripts issues are raised concerning the need for an ordained leader. As indicated in the previous chapter, most of the projects operate a 'shared leadership' function, where people are expected to participate in this form of leadership.

> In regards to services usually I work with 2 or 3 other people … who will head that up, and that encourages participation.[320]

However, at the same time, (and perhaps somewhat inconsistently), the same voices appear to recognise the need for a form of single leadership.

> I think it is a real strength having somebody as a leader who takes on and runs it as … We don't necessarily … have the political nous about the Anglican Church and nor the theological training ….[321]

It is true that in a post-Christendom and postmodern context, the role of the ordained leader needs to shift to skills of envisioner, empowerer, resourcer and facilitator.[322] However there also needs to be some form of visible governance structure where accountability is strongly identified. In any community project affecting the welfare of adults and children, there needs to be a system of saying 'No'. Yes, one that gives representation of all those involved, but one nevertheless that promotes some form of safety and boundaries. One of the transcripts promoted the group's vision of a fluid community where there is an active non-structure.

> Yes we love our flexibility and our organic identity … our non-existent, non-hierarchical … non-structure.[323]

Whilst there was a governance system in place through the planning group, respondents recognise that the visibility of this group was a credible concern.

> I think the problem with our approach is that some people find it difficult to know when they belong … Or simply they want more structure or defined control … Some people struggle … they do not know how they sit or where they sit if they come from that mind set that 'I need to find my place' … There are a few people … [who] find that quite difficult who want to be able to label … and put it in a box.[324]

In the transcripts of the same group, the leader identified a weakness with the group's governance structures required to resolve issues.

> In the three years or so in [the project] there have been two or three points of … conflict.[325]

It is further clear, that the Diocese had not formalised accountability structures:

> When the Diocese appointed me they didn't have an exact idea of what they wanted … With me it was appoint one person and see what happens, now that's great for the amount of freedom I get, but as the same time it means that the Diocese is … working on the hoof

to create structures ... The danger is that I could have gone off and done anything potentially, however it has worked well.[326]

If it was not for the excellent skills and integrity of the licensed leader, and a very skilled leadership team, this form of project governance could have led to significant problems.

This raises concerns about safety and governance of projects operating in a postmodern context. In such situations, there is a real danger that anyone with a charismatic persuasive personality can assume such leadership roles where the usual correctives, checks, balances and accountability, are not in place.[327] Such forms of charismatic leadership may challenge those licensed or ordained in situations of unclear governance structures. Equally, ordained leaders in situations of poor accountability can maximise their power and influence over and above what is usually acceptable or permissible in more traditional forms of Anglican Church. As Percy has stated this form of charismatic leadership in a postmodern fluid church context can raise significant problems around power abuse.

> The conditions of postmodernity however, have offered a new lease of life to the charismatic agent who can adapt to religious and cultural flux, mastering it and perhaps even 'surfing' the waves of renewal ... Charismatic authority is capable of competing with rational or traditional patterns of power: charisma derives its authority through the devotion it inspires and the benefits it brings to believers ...[328]

> Charismatic leadership is a form of domination and a method of power-exchange.[329]

Clearly this non-structural form of governance is not shared by the other groups. All the groups have an ordained and/or licensed church leader, authorised by the Diocesan Bishop. However, the very fact that people question the need for ordination, means that this concept of Anglican leadership is not understood or fully appreciated. As with the 'mystical communion model of Church' explored in Chapter Four, there are considerable weaknesses and potentials for power abuse if governance structures are not visible and explicit. In Anglicanism there is a clear understanding of what ordination stands for concerning authority and leadership:

The ordained minister is placed by ordination in a special relationship to the common priesthood, on behalf of the community of which [they] have pastoral charge. This is not a handing over of authority to be exercised by personal right, but an entrusting of responsibility answerable to Christ and to the community ... exercised from within the community and on its behalf, and thus it can have no independent authority. Such an office is not an open-ended gift of power, but an entrusting of authority for a limited purpose within the Koinonia, or fellowship.[330]

So the whole area of what ordained ministry means in the context of Fresh Expressions of Church is another important subject that needs further research that cannot be adequately explored here. Further, there is little clarity in the transcripts about the need to enable people involved in the various projects to discern a potential calling to the ordained ministry, leadership or other roles, other than group 'shared leadership' skills.

However, in other groups, there is clearer understanding of how the traditional governance structures relate to their particular church project.

We have three people on the Churches parish council... and through [our leader] ... who is an ordained deacon ... there is definite accountability and relationship there.[331]

Contextual Theology & A Theology of Presence

As was discussed earlier, Anglicanism has sought to use a process to guide ministry[332] (what has more recently been called orthopraxis) from its earliest days, which draws on the dialogue between Scripture, theology, the humanities, and culture. This is, by its very nature, a form of 'contextual theology' to guide right action. So, for the purpose of this study, contextual theology is an important focus for Anglicanism.[333] As Leech has said:

To be Anglican intelligently is to enter into a particular way of doing theology which brings together pastoral and academic approaches as well as socio-political struggle. This is true in spite of the immense differences in the way such theology is interpreted. Thus, at best, and clothed in their right mind, evangelicals, liberals, anglo-catholics, and all the people who do not fit these increasingly problematic labels, do tend to have in common a broad view of pastoral care, a respect for the intellect and for freedom of thought, and a commitment to some kind of involvement in the issues of wider society ... it is a major strength of the Anglican way.[334]

In the transcripts, one of the respondents articulated their frustration with having to 'check your brain in' at the door of some churches, and by implication co-started the Fresh Expression because they wanted intellectual freedom, and to take both pastoral and academic approaches to 'doing church'.[335] This further links to the exploration in Chapter Two, where it was identified that the projects in this study are using a synthetic approach to contextual theology. Further, their stance appears to be a 'both and' approach to the two over-riding theologies influencing contextual theology. Firstly redemptive theology, which tends to have a high regard towards Christ as God, and Holy Scripture, and a low regard towards experience and culture; and secondly, incarnational theology, which tends to have a high regard towards Christ as Human, experience and culture, and a low regard towards Christ as God and Holy Scripture.[336] Relating this back to Hooker's settlement of the 'conservative and the radical', the 'protestant and the catholic', the Fresh Expressions of Church in this study may be using such a 'both and' approach to contextual theology that sees the foot of the cross as the synthesis or fusion of both redemptive and incarnational theologies, which incidentally recognises Jesus' true identity as fully human and fully God. In this way, it may be that Fresh Expressions of Church have recovered a uniquely Anglican way of proceeding in a 'both and' approach to contextual theology. The transcripts give little evidence for this, probably because the questions and interviews were not geared towards this particular area of inquiry.

Closely linked to this Anglican approach to contextual theology is the Anglican theology of Presence which has been articulated as being:

> Our calling, is not to withhold our presence from those around us. Our calling, as imitators of Jesus Christ, is to bestow ourselves; to seek ever-new ways of being fully present to our brothers and sisters, and the people God gives us to share our lives with.[337]

This concept of presence returns to the Holy Trinity as perfect presence, and also to the words of Jesus in John chapters 15 and 17, where Jesus says to the disciples "Abide in me and I will abide in you", and (at the crucifixion) "Father glorify me in your presence".[338] This sense of Christ's presence in the body of Christ has profound missiological implications. Anglican Christians have a calling to share their lives with particular people, localities and places. This is an apostolic calling of being 'sent'. So the system of parishes, dioceses and provinces relates to this incarnational calling to have a presence with the ordinary people whom Anglican Christians live amongst. Everyone in the nation can turn to their local Anglican church, which by default seeks a presence with local people. Hence why the Church of England has chaplains and representatives in business, in shopping centres, in Government, in hospitals, in every conceivable area of public life. So practicing the presence of God with those who you relate to and live amongst is strongly Anglican.[339]

It is therefore no co-incidence, that each of the four projects specifically seeks to have such a presence in different places. In the centre of Birmingham, Manchester, Westminster, and in the Fremont area of Seattle. This is in fact so implicit to the function of two of the study projects, that part of their name relates to the local postcode (Sanctus 1 relating to the postcode area 1 for the city centre of Manchester, and B1 for the B1 postal area of Birmingham).[340] The missiological vision is profoundly relational and relates to postmodern forms of connection through relational networks, through events, through the internet and other information technology. This sense of presence relates to the core Anglican ideal of location and presence, that relates to place but also responds to new social ways of relating. In a time where public space, as a shared and interactive environment, is decreasing, at least one of the projects seeks to recreate public space and hence create a place for interconnection and dialogue. By setting up a café church, COTA seeks to provide a space for being Church, and as a catalyst of mission through relating:

> The Holy Spirit needs room to move and God needs to speak and God speaks and people interact with one another. It's personal ... relational. Space for relationality to happen. It isn't a programme for getting people to the church. It's a space for relationships to happen ... It is a positive presence ....[341]

Similarly Sanctus 1 hold a late night café for clubbers and people attending music gigs:

It is very much about 'sacred space' as well ... creating sacred space in the heart of a busy city centre ... A place where people can stop and connect with God. A place where they can come and just be.[342]

The Moot group also articulated their intention to develop activity in public space as a form of presence:

Some of the ideas behind Moot were for people to be able to access Christian spirituality in a public space, which I know we have done very little of, but I think certainly, that seemed to me to be one of the things that were at the heart of what Moot wanted to do.[343]

So this key function of Anglicanism as practicing the presence of God in every locality and area of public life is importantly central to the missiological calling of the four study groups, who further seek to create forms of public life and space.

Other Anglican flavours – Anglican Ancient-Future

When exploring Anglicanism as a word, the words 'ancient-future' were commonly used, which implies a belief in the value of tradition from ancient to recent, with all the resources this offers contemporary expressions of Church.[344]

I felt strongly when I started B1 that there was a whole collected Anglican tradition, liturgy and music out there that churches just do not touch. We have a liturgical framework but actually it's boring if it is not drawing on the treasure trove of our heritage. We said early on that we wanted to mix the best of the old and mix it with the best of the new. I think we have done that.[345]

Evaluation of the Projects against the Toyne report criteria for the new Pastoral Measure

Of the six set criteria in the Toyne Report, there are only two criteria that provide significant complication, while the other four have clearly been met;[346] The two criteria which remain problematic for the groups are:

(iv) They should include a distinctively Anglican component.

(v) They should normally be within synodical government structures;

Clearly (v) cannot be met until the pastoral measure reform has been completed to enable Fresh Expressions of Church to be legally recognised and included in binding governance structures. Unfortunately, the vagueness of (iv) makes it extremely difficult to make a definitive answer. For the purpose of this study, and the many resonances established in this chapter, the author's view is that each of the projects are drawing on and expressing a distinctive form of Anglicanism if by this the vision and values of Richard Hooker are representative of what it means to be authentically Anglican.

So to conclude this chapter, the political origins of the Anglican Church were first explored, along with contemporary interpretations of Richard Hooker. In his writings, the themes of unity in diversity, 'both and' as a form of pluralism, participation, an ecclesiology inspired by the Trinity, emerging forms of faith, and his desire for counter-fundamentalism, resonates with the vision of the emerging church component of Fresh Expressions of Church as outlined in Chapters One to Four.

An exploration of an Anglican understandings of the 'One Holy Catholic and Apostolic Church' made connections with the projects, although there was not a consistent understanding of the implication of having an Anglican identity, which appeared to be divided between negative and positive responses. The negative opinion appeared to be concerned with the more 'Christendom' expression of Anglican Churches. However, the positive voices identified that their communities were becoming more familiar with Anglican forms growing into the tradition. The transcripts gave evidence of collaboration at a Diocesan and local level, but failed to appreciate the international flavour of Anglicanism, other than the project in Seattle. All groups valued the liturgical and spiritual resources of the Anglican tradition and gave evidence of using such Anglican resources, utilising authorised forms of services. Recognition was given to the Anglican Triad/Quadrilateral, as a form of contextual theology that can respond to change and the complexity of life. General evidence within the transcripts appeared to meet the expectations of the Chicago-Lambeth Quadrilateral concerning Church practice.

Inquiry into the Anglican understanding of 'Apostolic' raised the issue of the ordained ordering of authority. Whilst the transcripts recognised the authority of Bishops, this was not so for Deacons and Priests. One opinion appeared to question the very foundation of ordination but inconsistently appeared at the same time to value hierarchical leadership. One project indicated the desire for a totally non-structured community, even when this posed real problems. Further, in this same project there appeared to be reduced accountability to the Diocese. This form of minimal governance raised issues concerning safe church practice in an age of postmodernity and potential power abuse. This form of governance was not supported in the other groups, which used processes of accountability.

Transcript evidence resonated with The Anglican polity of presence, particularly the focus on relational presence to localities. Regarding Anglicanism's sense of ancient and contemporary, many of the groups identified with the rich spiritual and liturgical resources of the tradition.

Finally, a quick review of the six criteria set by the Toyne Report identified that four out of the six criteria were met. Of the two that were not met, the first was restricted by current church law, and the second was so broad and (arguably) ill-defined that it was almost impossible to answer.

It is the contention therefore that this chapter offered sufficient evidence of the Anglican roots of the study groups to legitimate them being named 'distinctively Anglican'.

Chapter Six

Conclusions

Main Findings

A number of key themes have emerged in the 'what, why and how' the four study projects are legitimate 'Fresh Expressions' of church and Anglican. These include the following:

What are they?

- Terminology is still evolving. The main term used for this experimental form of church in the Church of England was 'fresh expressions' which appeared to have a further two sub-groupings with the headings 'inherited' and 'emerging' forms. However, there was no consensus on the use of this typology. The term 'liquid church' also approximated to the term 'fresh expressions'. However, there was agreement that a key purpose of 'fresh expressions' was to bridge the gap between contemporary culture and the church, that each generation had the responsibility to be church 'afresh' to their context.

- Internationally, 'emerging' forms of church appeared to predominantly include 'alternative worship', 'network' and 'café' churches. Most were started by local initiative, in a very 'bottom up' way. In the UK 'inherited' forms of 'fresh expressions' appeared to include 'cell', 'youth', 'church plants' and other forms. The four study projects identified with being 'emerging' rather than 'inherited' sub-forms of 'fresh expressions'.

- The main difference between the two sub-groupings appeared to relate to the form of contextual theology, where 'emerging forms' appeared to identify with a synthetic model, where 'inherited forms' appeared to identify with a 'translation' model. Further, that the two sub-groupings were attempting to be authentic forms of missionary church to different aspects of contemporary culture.

- Exploration of our current culture identified a complex fusion of the pre-modern, modern and postmodern co-existing in a time of cultural shift. There is a need for a 'mixed economy of church' as outlined in the 'Mission Shaped Church' report to relate to this cultural shift, with traditional parish church working in collaboration with fresh expressions. Analysis of 'emerging church' forms of contextual theology demonstrated that they were attempting to identify with the more postmodern elements of contemporary culture, rather than the more 'modern' or 'premodern' which appeared to be the focus for traditional and 'inherited' forms of church.

- Exploration of the vision of the 'Emerging church' identified a plurality of vision drawing on a the best of catholic and protestant theologies and church practice, with forms of church that empowered the laity to play a more active role in 'being church'.

- These 'emerging churches' therefore sought to be relevant church to postmodern aspects of culture defined by consumption, uncertainty, immediacy and individualism. Postmodernism was understood to be a cultural shift caused by increasingly 'postmodern sensibilities' drawing on philosophical post-structuralist thought, post-Christendom values, the sociological effects of liquid modernity, advances in information technology and economic globalisation. Postmodernity was found to be the epoch of time following the end of modernity but also the continuation of modernity.

Why do we need them?

- Church history provides evidence that the Church in the West has constantly reformed in response to cultural change. Fresh Expressions are part of this ongoing process.

- Recent trends suggest that traditional and inherited forms of church will be unable to meet the gap between Church and postmodern elements of contemporary culture. Exploration of the effect of the Christendom mindset revealed evidence that traditional and inherited forms of church have difficulty adjusting their values to a post-Christendom mindset, more resonant with postmodern aspects of contemporary culture. Therefore a collaborative 'mixed economy' that includes 'fresh expressions' will assist the Church in contextual mission to the postmodern elements of contemporary culture.

- Fresh expressions are able to respond to the opportunities and challenges of this form of contextual mission, namely, a renewed hunger for relating; new forms of spirituality resultant from information technology that engage with mysticism, new forms of communication, listening and dialogue through experiential events;

experience through the arts; engaging and reframing consumption; enthusiasm for experimentation; renewed interest in the relevance of ancient spirituality positive engagement with social change; renewal of public space and engagement with the stranger.

How are they being church?

- The transcripts give strong evidence of authentic ecclesiology.

- The four projects have strong connections with two of Dulles' models of church, primarily 'the church as mystical communion' and secondarily 'the church as sacrament'.

- Through these models there was a strong understanding of Trinitarian theology, and of the significance of the church as 'the body of Christ' and the 'ekklesia' as foundational principles of the New Testament, birthed in the primitive church and modelled on the image of the Godhead.

- These models had advantages and disadvantages. The main advantages included the ability to respond to social change, the ability to relate both catholic and evangelical expressions of church, and that the church when in worship can be seen as a form of the numinous, of God's presence. The main disadvantages were due to their fluid nature a difficulty in defining church. In high expressions of the mystical significance of the church, the church becomes too closely identified with being 'God' and risks abusing this position, and reducing responsibility among members of the church. The greatest difficulty with these models, concerns the understanding of church structures and leadership.

- Explorations of the credal marks of the church, showed that the project groups expressed appreciation for the need of 'One, Holy, catholic and Apostolic' church, but once again there were problems with interpreting leadership. However, there was a strong association with the values of the 'Priesthood of all believers' in how the groups modelled church.

- Concerning functional understanding of the church, it was established that all the projects balanced worship, mission and community activities to promote a healthy sense of spirituality.

- Evaluating the transcript information in conjunction with the values of the 'Missionary Church' identified in the Mission-Shaped Church report, it is clear that the projects meet all of the five values except empowering leaders and their development.

How are they being Anglican?

- Exploration of the contemporary interpretations of the writings of the Anglican Divine Richard Hooker identified themes of unity in diversity, 'both and' as a form of pluralism, participation, an ecclesiology inspired by the Trinity, emerging forms of faith, and his opposition to fundamentalism. These themes resonated strongly with the vision of the emerging church component of Fresh Expressions of Church as outlined in chapters one to four.

- An exploration of the particularly Anglican understandings of the 'One Holy Catholic and Apostolic Church' made further connections with the projects, although there was not a consistent understanding regarding an Anglican identity, about which there were negative and positive opinions. Negative opinion appeared concerned with the more 'Christendom' mindset and expression of some Anglican Churches. However, positive opinions expressed the view that their communities were becoming more familiar with Anglican forms, so were growing into the tradition.

- The transcripts gave evidence of real collaboration at a Diocese and local level, but failed to appreciate the international flavour of Anglicanism, other than the project in Seattle.

- All groups expressed positive views of the liturgical and spiritual resources of the tradition and gave evidence of using such Anglican resources, including keeping to authorised forms of Eucharistic services. Recognition was given to the Anglican Triad/Quadrilateral, as a form of contextual theology that can respond to change and the complexity of life. General evidence within the transcripts appeared to meet the expectations of the Chicago-Lambeth Quadrilateral concerning Church practice.

- Inquiry into the Anglican understanding of 'Apostolic' gave rise to an exploration of the Ordained ordering of authority. Whilst the transcripts appeared to recognise the authority of Bishops, there was evidence of serious questions regarding Deacons and Priests. One voice appeared to question the very foundation of ordination but inconsistently appeared to value hierarchical leadership.

- Exploration of one of the projects indicated the desire by some for a non-structured community, even when this posed real problems. Further, in this same project there appeared to be little structured accountability to the Diocese. This form of minimal governance raised issues concerning safe church practice in an age of postmodernity, which could result in power abuse and assumed levels of authority with little accountability. However this weakness was quickly recognised and structures were implemented. Other groups used forms of accountability.

- An exploration of the Anglican polity of presence made a number of resonances with the study groups. Transcripts evidenced a focus on relational presence to their chosen localities, which further resonated with some of Jesus' biblical sayings. Many of the groups identified with the rich spiritual and liturgical resources of the Anglican tradition.

- A review of the six criteria set by the Toyne Report, aimed at evaluating whether Fresh Expressions were legitimately Anglican, identified that four out of the six were met. Objective (v) was not possible because changes in the pastoral measure had not occurred, preventing participation within synodical governance, and it was not possible to know if objective (vi) was definitively answered. However evidence from the transcripts, suggests that the four study group have as much an 'Anglican component' as any other Anglican church.

To conclude, the author contends that evidence in chapters four and five of this study authenticates that the four study 'emerging church' projects and subgrouping of 'Fresh Expressions' are authentic forms of Christian church and are fully Anglican.

Evaluation of the proposed changes in the 'Pastoral Measure'

Reflecting back on the Toyne report, it is the opinion of the author that there is insufficient detail pertaining to Anglican identity. The comprehensive theological section is not fully included in the recommendations, particularly when trying to answer objective (vi) of the criteria set by the Toyne report, that 'They should include a distinctively Anglican component'.[347] As stated in chapter five, this is so broad that it is almost impossible to answer. However, it may be possible to deepen this criterion through a number of sub-criteria, that reflect the founding vision of Anglicanism by such writers such as Hooker, which offer real substance in our postmodern times. The place of plurality of church expression, theology drawing on the Trinity of God's identity, the polity of presence, the place of a church catholic and reformed, a theology of 'both and', the importance of collaboration and the place of the 'church-local' as the Diocese, a vision of the joined up 'body of Christ', the need for toleration and collaboration, and the possible place of intolerance with those who are intolerant as forms of fundamentalism. These issues of Anglican identity not only raise questions for 'Fresh Expressions' but for all forms of Anglican church, to re-formulate a common Anglican identity with post-Christendom sensibilities – something that appears to be sadly lacking in many 'Anglican' churches. As was identified by Leech, the Anglican church continues to have serious weaknesses through its continuing adherence to a 'Christendom mindset'.[348] It may be that the Toyne report proceeded as far as it could in reaching a consensual understanding of Anglicanism. This work may need to go back to the General Synod of the Church of England to be more explicit in finding a common sense of Anglican identity to assist the church face real reform that remains authentically Anglican. The vision of the emerging church articulated by Larson & Osborne may significantly contribute to a reframed post-Christendom Anglican ecclesiology and identity, given the number of resonances that exist with Hooker's writings and the 'Mission Shaped Church' report.[349] Such an articulated vision for the Anglican Church would assist the tradition to develop a future.

Comment on the 'Mission-Shaped' Church report

This report remains a foundational text for 'Fresh Expressions of church'. However, a lot more work needs to be completed, particularly in the area of catholic theology and in the areas of evidence and research to support the ongoing development of 'fresh expressions'. It is true that the report largely draws on the more evangelical wing of the Anglican church, but there is a significant place for the more catholic inspired 'fresh expressions' to find their place. The author hopes that this study will open up a number of different avenues for the new Archbishop's and Methodist 'Fresh expressions' Agency, particularly in the identified areas of further research. There are a number of new catholic inspired fresh expressions[350] whose project-type need to be included in the Fresh Expressions typology.[351]

Identified areas for further research

'Transcript-led-research' opened up a number of research areas that could not be explored due to the limitations of this study, these included:

- Exploration of how new forms of mystical spirituality arise out of advances in information technology in the UK context.

- How and with what do Fresh Expressions develop a distinctly Anglican identity in a post-Christendom and postmodern context?

- How do Fresh Expressions which are the product of ecumenical partnership, establish an Anglican identity?

- The place of the ordained ministry and more generally the place of leadership, its discernment and formation in the context of Anglican Fresh Expressions of church.

Evaluation of research methodology & outcome

The study methodology created a number of advantages and disadvantages that became apparent in completion of the research process.

- Firstly the criteria drawn from the Langrish typology set for the selection of the four study groups proved to be very reliable which enabled valuable narrative verbal data collection for this study. This data allowed a full exploration of the study question. However, the selection criteria did not reflect the two sub-groupings of 'fresh expressions' resulting in all four projects falling within the 'emerging church' subgrouping, and none within the 'inherited' forms. This made the data 'one-sided' and possibly over-critical of 'inherited' forms of Fresh Expressions of church. Inclusion of one 'inherited' form would have assisted in the exploration of a typology and the terminology covered in Chapter Two.

- The 'participatory action' and 'case study' approach in connection with the 'NAOMIE VC' process proved to be a very strong and effective way of eliciting the data required to explore the study question in dialogue with the relevant literature. It enabled a full exploration of points of connection and dis-connection relating to being 'church' and 'Anglican'. Further the approach prevented the researcher from manipulating and distorting the data, whilst enabling detailed clarification of questions due to the familiarity of the researcher with these forms of church. In particular, the author found the 'Moot' transcript to be at odds in many places with a lot of his own personal values and beliefs about the project and its purpose for which he was personally involved. The use of an external administrator to convert the recorded interviews into written transcripts removed any temptation of the researcher to tamper with results. However, the 'NAOMIE VC' informed questions did not allow for detailed exploration of contextual theology and the forms and perceptions of the ordained ministry. These are key areas when considering the study question.

- The use of MSN Messenger proved to be an effective tool in 'group-narrative' data collection to allow for clarifications and further questions pertaining to the chapter questions. As this facility removed the need for conversion to transcription, it proved to be an effective research tool, although discussion was slowed through the process of using the internet.

- The transcription process proved to be detailed and time consuming, but did enable collection of significant detail in a particular snap-shot-of-time.

Endnotes

1   A Porter, The Imperial Horizons of British Protestant Missions, 1880-1914 (Studies in the History of Christian Missions), (Cambridge: Eerdmans Publishing Company, 2003)..

2   Murray, Post-Christendom, 251-6.

3   P Harris et al Breaking New Ground: Church Planting in the Church of England, (London: Church House Publishing, 1994).

4   Harris, Breaking, v-vi. P Toyne et al A Measure for Measures: In mission and ministry. Report of the Review of the Dioceses, Pastoral Measure and related Measures, (London: Church House Publishing, 2004), ix.

5   G Cray et al, A Mission-Shaped Church Report, (London: Church House Publishing, 2004), vii, xi, 35.

6   Cray, A Mission, 84-102.

7   Cray, A Mission, 43-82.

8   'Lambeth Partners' is the name given to the group of financial donors who support the Charitable work of 'Lambeth Projects Limited' that seeks to resource aspects of the vision of the current Archbishop of Canterbury.

9   See "http://www.freshexpressions.org.uk".

10 R Williams, Presidential Address to General Synod, July 2003, retrieved 6th January 2004 from the World Wide Web, "http://www.archbishopofcanterbury.org/sermons_speeches/2003/030714.html".

11 Toyne, A Measure.

12 Toyne, A Measure, 32.

13 S Murray, Church Planting: Laying Foundations, (London: Paternoster Press, 1998), 31 in Cray, A Mission, 100.

14 Cray, A Mission, 99-102.

15 Toyne, A Measure, 4-5, 21-22, 31-33.

16 A non-UK equivalent 'fresh expression of church' project was chosen to assist with the question concerning 'being Anglican'.

17 Much has been written on the reliability of this method to gather 'first hand information', a full summary of these strengths are listed by D Garson Participant Observation, (New York: New York State University, 2004), retrieved 4th November 2004 from the World Wide Web, "http://www2.chass.ncsu.edu/garson/pa765/particip.htm".

18 J I Karlsen "Action Research as Method" in (ed) W Foote Whyte Participatory Action Research, (London: Sage Publications, 1991), 143-58.

19 A Jamieson A Churchless faith, (London: SPCK, 2002), 10.

20 J Langrish Case Studies as a Biological Research Process Research Paper 67, (Manchester: Manchester Metropolitan University Institute of Advanced Studies, 1993), 1.

21 Langrish, Case Studies, 1-12.

22 Garson, Participant Observation.

23 T May Social Research: Issues, Methods and Process, (Birmingham: Open University Press, 1993), 35, 49, 124-5. H M Collins "Researching Spoonbending: Concepts and practice of participatory fieldwork" in (eds) C Bell H Roberts Social Researching: Politics, problems, practice, (London: Routledge & Kegan Paul, 1984), 57. Karlsen, Action Research, 144.

24 May, Social Research, 37. Note: The researcher is currently completing a Curacy after being ordained in June 2004 to serve a title to St Matthew's Church, Westminster and the Moot Community.

25 R E Cole "Participant Observer Research" in Foote Whyte, Participatory, 159-166.

26 Garson, Participant, 162.

27 M Brown Many Mansions – Evaluating Church – Related Projects on Housing and Homelessness Occasional Paper 23, (Manchester: The William Temple Foundation, 1993), 3-4, 38. J Wood The Naomie Planning Model, (Chingford: Youth work Central, 2000), 1 as retrieved 3rd September 2004 from the World Wide Web, "http:// youthworkcentral.tripod.com/naomie.htm". Anon Managing Change Item Code:FS310602, (Chingford: The Scout Association Information Centre, 2000), 3. Anon Systematic Approach to Planning Item Code: FS140036, (Chingford: The Scout Association Information Centre, 1996), 1.

28 Anon, Systematic Approach, 1-2.

29 Brown, Many, 3-4, 38.

30 See Appendix 2 for the list of agreed questions for the interviews. Note: Initial 'NAOMIE VC' questions were trialled with two respondents outside of the study groups who were involved in 'fresh expressions of church', and modified to reduce jargon and improve plain English.

31 Groups that had a good reputation and were well known in and outside 'emerging church' and 'fresh expressions' circles. Such groups were more likely to participate

and not terminate before the completion of the research process.

32 Groups who had individual members that were known outside the group, and who had responded to email and letter communication reliably. Without this, practical completion of the research phase would have been difficult.

33 This criteria aimed to only include projects that were relevant to the research question.

34 Langrish, Case Studies, 7-8. Brown, Many, 1.

35 See Appendix 1 for a copy of the letter sent to participants.

36 Appendix 8, 179.

37 Note: The five transcripts are compiled into appendices 4-8.

38 Appendix 7, 170-1, Appendix 5, 134-5, Appendix 4, 114-5, 120, Appendix 6, 156-7.

39 P Bayes Mission-Shaped Church, (Cambridge: Grove Books Ltd, 2004), 8. Note: This declaration is put to all clergy at ordination and to Lay Workers and Readers whenever they are licensed to new work.

40 Cray, A Mission, 33-4.

41 See Context section later.

42 K Brewin The Complex Christ, Signs of emergence in the urban church, (London: SPCK, 2004), 23-4.

43 As retrieved 14th August 2005 from the World Wide Web, "http://www.google.co.uk" and "http://www.emergingchurch.info/about/index.htm".

44 S Murray Church after Christendom, (London: Paternoster Press, 2004), 73.

45 P Ward Liquid Church, (Carlisle: Pater Noster Press, 2002), 2,15-6. Note, this term also relates to Z Bauman's concept of 'liquid modernity', see later.

46 B Larson, R Osbourne The emerging church, (London: Word Books, 1970), 9-11.

47 Cray, A Mission, 33-4.

48 R Warren Being Human Being Church, (London: Marshall Pickering, 1995), 37-51, 83-98.

49 Warren, Being, 30-36, 41-3. Note: Warren's use of 'inherited church' also correlates Ward's use of 'solid church' to describe the form of church within a modern cultural paradigm. Ward, Liquid Church, 29-30.

50 Murray, Church, 73-4. M Riddell Threshold to the Future, (London: SPCK, 1998), 14-5, 28-9.

51 Note: A number of writers including Warren are particularly critical of leadership of forms of 'inherited' or 'solid' church as having a tendency towards being fixed,

unwieldy, and hierarchical. That their mission and pastoral care tends to be inward looking and focused on keeping people happy rather than on mission, faith formation or development. See Warren, Being, 32-33.

52 E Farley Deep Symbols: Their Postmodern Effacement and Reclamation, (Valley Forge, USA: Trinity Press, 1996), 12.

53 A Shanks God and Modernity, a new and better way to do theology, (London: Routledge, 2000), 18-24.

54 R Horner Jean-Luc Marion, A Theo-logical Introduction, (Aldershot: Ashgate, 2005), 14-5.

55 Ibid. M P Gallagher, Clashing Symbols An Introduction to Faith & Culture, (London: DLT, 2003), 104-10.

56 Horner, Jean-Luc, 16. Gallagher, Clashing, 106-10.

57 M Percy Power & The Church: Ecclesiology in an Age of Transition, (London: Continuum, 1998), 220. Brewin, Complex, 6.

58 Gallagher, Clashing, 100-4.

59 Poststructural thinking tends to resist the limitation of meaning by focusing on the irreducibility particular, rather than the universal. Structuralism focused on looking for evidence in situations to find universal principles. Poststructualism challenges the authenticity of the scientific method as a reliable vehicle for meaning – stating that nothing can ever be truly objective. Horner, Jean -Luc, 17-8.

60 These values relate to a church that is increasingly disestablished in everything but name, which distances itself from the forms of power and authority exercised in Christendom, rejecting imperialistic language and cultural imposition. See chapter three for a fuller exploration of these values. Murray, Post-Christendom, 228-30.

61 See exploration of social context pages 20-4.

62 Late Global capitalism approximates to the time and effect of the expansion of global market economics and the erosion of social welfare provision, the instability of reliable work, and changes in corresponding family and social life. This is explored more fully in pages 20-4.

63 Horner, Jean-Luc, 15-6.

64 J Milbank, Theology and Social Theory: Beyond Secular Reason, (Oxford: Blackwell, 1990), 1-8, 65, 278-326.

65 J Bartley, Faith in politics after Christendom: the church as a movement for anarchy. (London: Paternoster, 2006), 29. S Murray "Rethinking atonement after Christendom" in (eds) S Barrow & J Bartley Consuming Passion, Why the killing of

Jesus really matters, (London: SLT, 2005), 32. Gallagher, Clashing, 100-4.

66 Z Bauman, Globalization The Human Consequences, (Oxford: Polity Press, 1998), 3-4.

67 Cray, A Mission, 33-4.

68 Ward, Liquid, 2,15.

69 Ward, Liquid, 38-9.

70 Murray, Church, 70-1.

71 J Baker "Ritual As Strategic Practice" in (ed) P Ward The Rite Stuff, (Oxford: BRF, 2004), 95. S Taylor A New Way of Being Church: A Case Study Approach to Cityside Baptist Church as Christian Faith 'making do' in a Postmodern World. A Doctorate Thesis, (Dunedin, New Zealand: University of Otago, 2005), 227-254. Riddell, Threshold, 12-13. Ward, Rite, 24-29. A Draper "Curiosity…Gave the Cat nine lives" in Ward, Rite, 67. G Lynch After Religion, (Wandsworth: DLT, 2000), 120.

72 See Appendix 7,164-5, Appendix 5, 127-9, Appendix 4, 110-2, Appendix 6, 159-61.

73 Murray, Church, 69-70.

74 Murray, Church, 74.

75 B Appleyard Understanding the Present: An Alternative History of Science, (London: Tauris Parke, 1995), 214, in Warren, Being, 44-5. R Williams Lost Icons Reflections on Cultural Bereavement, (London: T&T Clark, 2000), 144, 151. Warren, Being, 41-7. Riddell, Threshold, 101-14. D Lyon Jesus in Disneyland, Religion in Postmodern times (Oxford: Polity Press, 2002), 5, 12-4. Cray, A Mission, 9-10.

76 S Taylor The out-of-bounds church? Learning to create communities of faith in a culture of change, (Grand Rapids, USA: Zondervan, 2005), 24-7, 88. Z Bauman Liquid Modernity, (Oxford: Polity Press, 2000), 1-14, 53-63, 92.

77 Cray, A Mission, 1-4.

78 Lyon, Disneyland, 13-4, 37. J Caputo On Religion, Thinking In Action, (London: Routledge, 2001), 67-8, 76-7.

79 Bauman, Liquid, 6-15.

80 Cray, A Mission, 4. Warren, Being, 47-8.

81 Cray, A Mission, 4-7. M Castells The rise of the network society, (Oxford: Blackwell, 2000), 164. SJ Grenz "Ecclesiology" in (ed) KJ Vanhoozer The Cambridge Companion to Postmodern Theology, (Cambridge: CUP, 2003), 252-3.

82 Lynch, After, 3-9.

83 P Richter Gone but not forgotten, (London: DLT, 1998) in Cray, A Mission, 37-8.

84 Cray, A Mission, 39. A Jamieson A Churchless faith, (London: SPCK), 9,16.

85 Powerpoint presentation by Bishop Graham Cray in October 2005 to the 'Anglican Network Church Conference' entitled 'Reaching a Post-Modern Generation & the challenge of fresh expressions of church'.

86 Lyon, Disneyland, 140,142,148.

87 Lyon, Disneyland, 14.

88 Ward, Liquid, 15-6.

89 M McCarthy "Spirituality in a Postmodern Era" in J Woodward S Pattison A Blackwell Reader in Pastoral & Practical Theology, (Oxford: Blackwell, 1999), 192-205. Bauman, Liquid, 14, 178.

90 Taylor, Out, 81-3. J Drane "New Spirituality And Christian Mission" in The Bible in Transmission Summer 2005, (Swindon: Bible Society, 2005), 5-7. C Partridge "Alternative Spiritualities, Occulture and the re-enchantment of the West" in The Bible in Transmission Summer 2005, (Swindon: Bible Society, 2005), 2-5.

91 Caputo, On, 72-5.

92 See Appendices 4-7.

93 M Riddell God's home page, (London: Bible Reading Fellowship, 1998), 9-10.

94 Caputo, On, 90-92.

95 Williams, Presidential Address. Bayes, Mission-Shaped, 10. Cray, A Mission, xi-xii, 12-3, 35-6.

96 Appendix 8, 179. Note: website refers to http://www.freshexpressions.co.uk.

97 Appendix 8, 180.

98 Murray, Church, 70.

99 Brewin, Complex, 70.

100 Note: See Chapter 3 for a fuller description and exploration of these concepts as understood within this study.

101 Appendix 8, 179.

102 SB Bevans, Models of Contextual Theology, (New York: Orbis, 2002), 1-2,5,7.

103 Ibid, 1.

104 R Welch "Church Planting: A historical perspective" in (ed) S Timmis Reaching Today's Communities Through Church Planting, (Fearn, Ross-Shire: Christian Focus Publishing, 2000), 47-67. T Thornborough "Church Planting: Contemporary Initiatives in the UK" in Timmis, Reaching, 76-7.

105 Murray, Church, 69.

106 Note: Niebuhr defined five different models of how church relates to culture. Each hold varying theological and philosophical assumptions. He described culture as an 'artificial, secondary environment which humanity imposes on 'the natural', comprising 'language, habits, ideas, beliefs, customs, social organisation, inherited artefacts, technical processes and values". The model 'Christ against culture' draws on the doctrine of original sin, and the 'fallen-ness' of humanity, hence the need to prevent culture influencing the church. H R Niebuhr Christ and culture, (New York: Harper & Row, 1951), 30-9 in M Percy, The Salt of the Earth: Religious resilience in a Secular Age, (London: Continuum, 2002), 38-41, 49, 52-7.

107 Bevans, Models, 30-46.

108 Murray, Post-Christendom 200-206.

109 A Walker Restoring the Kingdom. The Radical Christianity of the House Church Movement, (Guildford: Eagle, 1998), 129-133, 147, 167-170.

110 B A Harvey Another City. (Harrisburg: Trinity Press International, 1999), 14.

111 It is assumed that the summary of 'emerging church' by Larson and Osborne and the stated general values of 'emerging church' are an accurate description.

112 Bevans, Models, 86.

113 Bevans, Models, 81-96.

114 Murray, Post-Christendom, 251-6.

115 Niebuhr, Christ and culture, in Percy, The Salt, 36-40.

116 Brewin, Complex 70.

117 Brewin, Complex, 16-17, 69-73.

118 Brewin, Complex, 52-4, 75-8. S Johnson Emergence, (London: Penguin, 2001), 15-21.

119 Brewin, Complex, 52-60.

120 Appendix 8, 180-1.

121 WA Clebesch CR Jaekle Pastoral Care in Historical Perspective, (London: Aronson, 1994), 1-4, 11-14.

122 HMSO, Belonging to a Religion: Social Trends 32, (London: HMSO, 2000), as retrieved 30th October 2005 from the World Wide Web, "http://www.statistics.gov.uk/STATBASE/ssdataset.asp?vlnk=5203".

123 Note: The reliability and validity of these statistics are not clearly established. Results do draw on questionnaires completed in 2005 on a percentage data set, sent out to Churches in the UK, but should not be treated as being as reliable as Government

Statistics.

124 P Brierley (ed) The Future of the Church: Religious Trends 5, (London: Christian Research, 2005). J Petre Churches 'on road to doom if trends continue', The Telegraph 3rd September 2005 as retrieved 30th October 2005 from the World Wide Web, "http://www.telegraph.co.uk/news/main.jhtml?xml=/news/2005/09/03/nchurch03.xml".

125 See G Davie Research 2005 recent media coverage, (London: Church of England, 2005) as retrieved 30th October 2005 from the World Wide Web, "http://www.cofe.anglican.org/info/statistics/".

126 L Barley Church of England Attendance figures 2003, (London: Research & Statistics for the Archbishops' Council, Church of England, 2003) as retrieved 30th October 2005 from the World Wide Web, "http://www.cofe.anglican.org/news/pro106.html" and "http://www.cofe.anglican.org/info/statistics/provisional_attendance_2003.pdf".

127 Harvey, Another City, 7-14. Murray, Post-Christendom, 83-88. S Murray "Rethinking atonement after Christendom" in (eds) S Barrow J Bartley Consuming Passion, Why the killing of Jesus really matters, (London: SLT, 2005), 32.

128 Warren, Being Human, 23-31. Harvey, Another City, 7-15. Murray, Post-Christendom, 83-88, 200-2.

129 Murray, Post-Christendom, 20-1. R C W Chartres Ecclesiology – Edmonton Area Conference 15-vi-2004, as retrieved from the World Wide Web on 7th January 2006 at "http://www.klisia.net/blog/BishopoflondonaddressEcclesiology-EdmontonAreaConference.15-vi-2004.pdf". Riddell, Threshold, 1-5, 11.

130 Riddell, Threshold, 12-15. Murray, Rethinking, 29. J Baker Ritual in Ward The Rite, 86-7.

131 Murray, Post-Christendom, 20-1, 229.

132 J Bartley Faith, chapter 1.

133 Note: These findings about de-churched factors relate to the national statistics for dechurched people in the UK in chapter 2. Jamieson, A Churchless, 16.

134 Appendix 8, 181.

135 Appendix 7, 166.

136 Appendix 4, 110-1.

137 Appendix 5, 130.

138 Appendix 6, 152.

139 Appendix 7, 164.

140 Grenz, Ecclesiology, 252-3.

141 Warren, Being, 16.

142 Greenwood in Warren, Being, 16.

143 Appendix 4, 115.

144 Grenz, Ecclesiology, 253.

145 Grenz, Ecclesiology, 256, 257.

146 Grenz, Ecclesiology, 252.

147 Cray, A Mission shaped, 82.

148 Appendix 7, 165.

149 M Brown "Whose Church? Which Culture?: Discerning the Missionary Structures for Tomorrow" in Toyne, A Measure, 122-3.

150 A Aven The Emerging Church According to Anna, (Winchester, USA: deepsoil, 2004), as retrieved 25th September 2004 from the World Wide Web "http://annaaven. typepad.com/emerging/2004/04/the_emerging_ch.html".

151 See chapter Two for an exploration on liquid modernity as a social context for 'Fresh Expressions', particularly the subgrouping of 'Emerging Church'.

152 Riddell God's home, 10.

153 Bauman, Modernity, 178.

154 Caputo, On, 67-8.

155 Caputo, On, 73.

156 Caputo, On, 70.

157 P J Rollins His Colour is Our Blood: A phenomenological of the prodigal Father, A PhD thesis, (Belfast: Queen's University, 2004), 117-20. E Davis, TechGnosis, Myth, Magic and Mysticism in the Age of Information, (London: Serpents Tail, 2004), 4-10.

158 Davis, TechGnosis, 5.

159 Davis, TechGnosis, 122.

160 Appendix 6, 160.

161 Appendix 4, 115.

162 Caputo, On, 92-3, 108.

163 Percy, The Salt, 165.

164 Warren, Being, 49.

165 Appendix 4, 112.

166 J Baker, Ritual, in Ward, The Rite, 95.

167 Taylor, Out, 91.

168 Appendix 7, 167.

169 Appendix 7, 168.

170 Appendix 4, 114.

171 Appendix 7, 166. See also Appendix 7, 168.

172 Warren, Being, 16-17.

173 Appendix 5, 132-3.

174 Taylor, Out, 35-7.

175 Appendix 8, 181.

176 See "http://www.moot.uk.net http://www.sanctus1.co.uk, http://b1.mychurchwebsite.co.uk/, http://www.apostleschurch.org", Appendix 5, 131-4, Appendix 4, 115.

177 Taylor, Out, 49, 55.

178 J Gladwin Love and Liberty: Faith and Unity in a Postmodern Age, (London: DLT, 1998), 209 in M Frost A Hirsch, The Shaping of Things to Come, (Peabody, Massachusetts: Hendrickson), 22.

179 Appendix 4, 118, 120-5, Appendix 5, 129, 132-3, 137-40, Appendix 6, 151-3, 155, 157-8, 163, Appendix 7, 165-7, 172.

180 P J Palmer The Company of Strangers, Christians and the renewal of America's Public Life, (New York: Crossroad, 1983), 1-25.

181 Ibid, 22-3.

182 Appendix 7, 167-70, Appendix 4, 116-7, Appendix 5, 127-9, 147, Appendix 6, 151-4.

183 Appendix 5, 136.

184 See Appendix 9 for a copy of this icon.

185 Appendix 7, 166, 169.

186 Appendix 6, 157.

187 Understood as the 'round dance of the Trinity'.

188 J M Tillard, Dilemmas of Modern Religious Life, (Delaware: Michael Glazier, 1984) in Grenz, Ecclesiology, 268.

189 Grenz, Ecclesiology, 268.

190 Ward, Liquid, 54.

191 M Volf, After Our Likeness The Church as the Image of the Trinity, (Cambridge: Eerdmans, 1998), 128-9, 208.

192 Volf, After, 128-9.

193 Volf, After, 208.

194 Volf, After, 235.

195 Brown, Whose, 107-8.

196 Appendix 5, 136.

197 Taylor, Out, 71.

198 J H Yoder The Priestly Kingdom: Social Ethics as Gospel, (Notre Dame, Indiana: University of Notre Dame Press, 1984), 91, in Harvey, Another, 27.

199 A Dulles Models of the Church, (New York: Bantam Doubleday Dell Publishing Group Inc, 1991), 40-55.

200 Dulles, Models, 40-4.

201 See next section.

202 Dulles, Models, 50.

203 Dulles, Models, 42-46, 50.

204 Dulles, Models 46, 50-1.

205 Cray, A Mission, 81-2, Bayes, Mission-Shaped, 12.

206 Dulles, Models, 44-53.

207 The author is unsupportive of this criticism of the study projects, which sincerely aim to shape church into the culture in which they are located.

208 Appendix 4, 121.

209 Appendix 5, 142.

210 Ward, Liquid, 33-9.

211 Appendix 4, 115.

212 Appendix 6, 153.

213 Ward, Liquid, 6-9. Harvey, Another, 150.

214 Grenz, Ecclesiology, 257-60.

215 Harvey, Another, 15-6, 25.

216 Chartres, Ecclesiology, 2-3.

217 P Avis The Anglican Understanding of Church, (London: SPCK, 2000),1. Harvey, Another, 23.

218 Chartres, Ecclesiology, 2-3. M Maggay Transforming Society, (Oxford: Lynx, 1994), 31-3, 36-7, 49-50.

219 Harvey, Another City, 17-22. Ward, Liquid, 9-10.

220 Chartres, Ecclesiology, 3. Harvey, Another, 57. Maggay, Transforming, 15.

221 G Florovsky in Harvey, Another, 21-2.

222 Appendix 4, 120-1.

223 Appendix 7, 170.

224 Harvey, Another, 57, 150.

225 Chartres, Ecclesiology, 3.

226 Appendix 8, 184-5.

227 Dulles, Models, 55-63.

228 Dulles, Models, 60-3.

229 See Appendix 9.

230 Appendix 8, 185.

231 Cray, A Mission, 81. Bayes, Mission-Shaped, 12.

232 Brown, Whose, 108.

233 Appendix 8, 183.

234 Brown, Whose, 109-10. Chartres, Ecclesiology, 5.

235 Appendix 8, 184.

236 Appendix 4, 123.

237 Appendix 5, 142.

238 Appendix 6, 159.

239 Brown, Whose, 110-1.

240 Appendix 5, 139.

241 Appendix 8, 179.

242 Appendix 8, 181.

243 Brown, Whose, 111-2. Avis, The Anglican, 65-66, 72.

244 Appendix 4, 123.

245 Brown, Whose, 112-3. Avis, The Anglican, 72. Grenz, Ecclesiology, 267.

246 As identified as the Church as 'One' and 'catholic'.

247 See 'Challenges' section and next chapter.

248 Appendix 4, 110-1.

249 Appendix 7, 164-5, Appendix 6, 149-51, Appendix 5, 127-9.

250 Appendix 8, 184.

251 Appendix 5, 140.

252 Appendix 7, 165.

253 Appendix 5, 141.

254 Cray, A Mission, 81. Bayes, Mission-Shaped, 12.

255 Warren, Being, 88-92. Toyne, A Measure, 22.

256 See the project transcripts in the appendices.

257 Bayes, Mission-Shaped, 12. Cray, A Mission, 82.

258 Note: In the author's experience, there have been a few Methodist, Baptist and

United Reformed Church new forms, but the vast majority have connections to Anglican and Episcopal Churches in the UK.

259 O Chadwick The Reformation, (London: Penguin, 1990), 384-5, 389-90.

260 J Morris "The Future of Church and State" in D Dormor, J McDonald, J Caddick, Anglicanism The Answer to Modernity. (London: Continuum, 2003), 164.

261 M Percy, Introducing Richard Hooker and the Laws of Ecclesiastical Polity, (London: DLT, 1999), 9-11. Avis, The Anglican, 11-3.

262 Brown, Whose, 114. G R Evans Authority in the Church: A Challenge for Anglicans, (Norwich: Canterbury Press, 1994), 4.

263 Percy, Introducing, 9-11. Avis, The Anglican, 11

264 Note: Polity relates to 'governance'.

265 Percy, Introducing, 12, 18.

266 Percy, Introducing, 17, 19.

267 R Hooker Of the Laws of Ecclesiastical Polity, as reproduced in modern language in (ed) A S McGrade Of the Laws of Ecclesiastical Polity Preface, Book I and Book VIII, Cambridge Texts in the History of Political Thought, (Cambridge: CUP, 1989), the First Book [1.3], 2.

268 B McLaren A Generous Orthodoxy, (Grand Rapids: Zondervan, 2004), 209-10.

269 This criticism fails to understand how Anglicanism seeks to be 'One', explored in chapter 4 and later in this chapter.

270 Percy, Introducing, 27.

271 Percy, Introducing, 42-3.

272 Percy, Introducing, 29, 31, 53.

273 Percy, Introducing, 21-22.

274 Hooker, Of, the First book [2.2-2.3], 55.

275 Hooker, Of, the Eighth book [6.4], 182.

276 Percy, Introducing, 29.

277 R Thompson, Is there an Anglican Way? Scripture, Church and Reason: New Approaches to an Old Triad, (London: DLT, 1997), 41.

278 Thompson, Is there, 24-5.

279 Thompson, Is there, 22-3.

280 Percy, Introducing, 12, 23.

281 Note: which were either radical Protestantism or Roman Catholicism.

282 Avis, The Anglican, 52.

283 Appendix 4, 124.

284 The words 'Baptist', 'Charismatic Evangelical' and 'Conservative Evangelical' were used in the transcripts as churches respondents had previously participated in.

285 Appendix 4, 117-8, 124, Appendix 5, 135, 145-6, Appendix 6, 159-60.

286 Appendix 4, 123.

287 K Leech, The Sky is Red, Discerning the signs of the times, (London: DLT, 1997), 58-9.

288 Appendix 6, 161.

289 Avis, The Anglican, 77.

290 Evans, Authority, 2. Brown, Whose, 115.

291 Brown, Whose, 115.

292 Appendix 4, 121-4, Appendix 5, 147, Appendix 6, 151-2, 160-2, Appendix 7, 166-8.

293 Appendix 5, 145-6, Appendix 6, 160-1.

294 Appendix 4, 123.

295 Appendix 4, 123.

296 Appendix 6, 160-1.

297 Appendix 4, 121-2, Appendix 5, 144-5, Appendix 7, 173.

298 Appendix 4, 122-3.

299 Appendix 6, 161.

300 Evans, Authority, 2-3.

301 Evidence for this is listed on the COTA website where it states membership of the Anglican Communion and uses the Anglican Communion logo as retrieved 16th January 2005 from "http://www.apostleschurch.org" and as discussed on the group blog as retrieved 16th January 2005 from the World Wide Web, "http://www.submergence.org".

302 Appendix 7, 172-3, Appendix 6, 159-60, Appendix 5, 131, 139, Appendix 4, 119, Appendix 8, 184-7.

303 Appendix 5, 139, Appendix 6, 160-1.

304 Appendix 7, 172-3, Appendix 8, 175, Appendix 4, 118-9, Appendix 5, 129, 139-40, Appendix 6, 152, 158.

305 Appendix 4, 119, Appendix 8, 183-4.

306 Appendix 5, 134-5, 147-8, Appendix 7, 164, 166-7.

307 Percy, Introducing, 22.

308 Evans, Authority, 14.

309 It should be noted that in initial writing by Hooker, that 'Reason' was placed before

'Tradition', in other adaptations the word 'Church' was used instead of 'tradition'. Experience has further been swapped for the word 'cultural experience' or 'culture'. Percy, Introducing 22. Thompson, Is there 4-5.

310 Evans, Authority, 7.

311 Evans, Authority, 2, 15. McLaren, A Generous, 209-10.

312 Brown, Whose, 115.

313 Appendix 8, 185.

314 Evans, Authority, 90.

315 Appendix 4, 119, and the project websites: 'http://www.moot.uk.net', 'http://www.sanctus1.co.uk', 'http://www.churchoftheapostles.org', 'http://b1.mychurchwebsite.co.uk'.

316 Avis, The Anglican, 52.

317 Ibid, 19-20.

318 Appendix 5, 144, Appendix 6, 161-2, Appendix 4, 119, 121-2, Appendix 7, 164, 166-7.

319 Appendix 5, 148.

320 Appendix 5, 141.

321 Appendix 5, 148.

322 W Brueggemann Israel's Praise Doxology against Idolatry, (Philadelphia: Fortress Press, 1988), 26-8.

323 Appendix 5, 137, 140.

324 Appendix 5, 137-8, 140.

325 Appendix 5, 143.

326 Appendix 5, 146. Note: Since completing the research, these issues have been identified and addressed by the creation of a formal planning group alongside more formal accountability structures to the Diocese.

327 As clearly happened with the Nine O'clock Service in Sheffield.

328 Percy, Power, 11-12.

329 Ibid, 12.

330 Evans, Authority, 23.

331 Appendix 6, 160.

332 'Scripture, reason, tradition & experience'.

333 This position was articulated strongly by 'Person 2' in Appendix 4, 124.

334 Leech, The Sky, 59.

335 Appendix 5, 127.

336 The author has explored this 'both and' theology for the emerging church as a published article. I Mobsby, Is there a distinctive approach to theologising for the emerging church?, as published 1ˢᵗ October 2005 on the World Wide Web, "http://www.emergingchurch.info/reflection/ianmobsby/theology.htm".

337 B Quash, "The Anglican Church as a Polity of Presence" in Dormor, Anglicanism The Answer, 38-9.

338 Ibid, 41-2.

339 Ibid, 42-51, 53, 56.

340 Appendix 4, 116, Appendix 5, 127-8, 147, Appendix 7, 166-9.

341 Appendix 7, 169-70.

342 Appendix 5, 133, 139.

343 Appendix 6, 153.

344 Appendix 8, 185, Appendix 5, 131, 139, Appendix 6, 160, Appendix 7, 172-3.

345 Appendix 4, 119.

346 See page 3 for the full list of expectations.

347 See Page 3.

348 See Page 73.

349 See Page 15.

350 Particularly in the Diocese of Oxford.

351 See Page 2.

Bibliography

Anon   (2000) Managing Change Item Code:FS310602. Chingford: The Scout Association Information Centre.

Anon   (1996) Systematic Approach to Planning Item Code: FS140036. Chingford: The Scout Association Information Centre.

Aven   (2004) The Emerging Church According to Anna. As retrieved September 25th 2004 from the World Wide Web, "http://annaaven.typepad.com/emerging/2004/04/the_emerging_ch.html".

Avis P   (2000) The Anglican Understanding of Church. London: SPCK.

Baker J   (2004) "Ritual As Strategic Practice" in (ed) Ward P The Rite Stuff. Oxford: BRF.

Barley L   (2003) Church of England Attendance figures 2003. London: Research & Statistics for the Archbishops' Council, Church of England, as retrieved 30th October 2005 from the World Wide Web, "http://www.cofe.anglican.org/news/pro106.html" and "http://www.cofe.anglican.org/info/statistics/provisional_attendance_2003.pdf".

Barrow S Bartley J (eds) (2005) Consuming Passion, Why the killing of Jesus really matters. London: DLT.

Bartley J   Faith in politics after Christendom: the church as a movement for anarchy. London: Paternoster.

Bayes P   (2004) Mission-Shaped Church. Cambridge: Grove Books Ltd.

Bauman Z   (1998) Globalization The Human Consequences. Oxford: Polity Press.

Bauman Z   (2000) Liquid Modernity. Oxford: Polity Press.

Bevans SB   (2002) Models of Contextual Theology. New York: Orbis.

Brierley P (ed)   (2005) The Future of the Church: Religious Trends 5. London: Christian Research.

Brewin K   (2004) The Complex Christ, Signs of emergence in the urban church. London: SPCK.

Brown M   (1993) Many Mansions – Evaluating Church – Related Projects on Housing and Homelessness Occasional Paper 23. Manchester: The William Temple Foundation.

Brown M   (2004) "Whose church? Which Culture?: Discerning the Missionary Structures for Tomorrow, Appendix I" in Toyne P et al (2004) A Measure for Measures: In mission and ministry. Report of the Review of the Dioceses, Pastoral Measure and related Measures. London: Church House Publishing, 107-28.

Brueggemann W (1988) Israel's Praise Doxology against Idolatry. Philadelphia: Fortress Press.

Caputo JD   (2001) On Religion, Thinking In Action. London: Routledge.

Castells M   (2000) The rise of the network society. Oxford: Blackwell.

Chadwick O   (1990) The Reformation. London: Penguin.

Chartres RCW (2004) Ecclesiology – Edmonton Area Conference 15-vi-2004, as retrieved 7th January 2006 from the World Wide Web, "http://www.klisia.net/blog/BishopoflondonaddressEcclesiology-EdmontonAreaConference.15-vi-2004.pdf".

Clebesch WA Jaekle CR (1994) Pastoral Care in Historical Perspective. London: Aronson.

Cole RE   (1991) "Participant Observer Research" in (ed) Foote Whyte W Participatory Action Research. London: Sage Publications, 159-166.

Collins HM   (1984) "Researching Spoonbending: Concepts and practice of participatory fieldwork" in (eds) Bell C Roberts H Social Researching: Politics, problems, practice. London: Routledge & Kegan Paul, 54-69.

Cray G et al   (2004) A Mission-Shaped Church Report. London: Church House Publishing.

Davis E   (2004) TechGnosis, Myth, Magic and Mysticism in the Age of Information. London: Serpents Tail.

Dormor D, McDonald J, Caddick J (2003) Anglicanism The Answer to Modernity. London: Continuum.

Drane J   (2005) "New Spirituality And Christian Mission" in The Bible in Translation, Summer 2005. Swindon: Bible Society.

Dulles A   (1991) Models of the Church. New York: Bantam Doubleday Dell Publishing Group Inc.

Evans GR   (1994) Authority in the Church: A Challenge for Anglicans. Norwich: Canterbury Press.

Farley E   (1996) Deep Symbols: Their Postmodern Effacement and Reclamation. Valley Forge, USA: Trinity Press.

Foote Whyte W (ed) (1991) Participatory Action Research. London: Sage Publications.

Frost M Hirsch A (2004) The Shaping of Things to Come. Peabody, Massachusetts: Hendrickson.

Gallagher MP   (2003) Clashing Symbols An Introduction to Faith & Culture. London: DLT.

Garson D	(2004) Participant Observation. New York: New York State University as retrieved 4th November 2004 from the World Wide Web, "http://www2.chass.ncsu.edu/garson/pa765/particip.htm".

Garson D   (2004) Participant Observation.
New York: New York State University as retrieved 4th November 2004 from the World Wide Web, "http://www2.chass.ncsu.edu/garson/pa765/particip.htm".

Grenz SJ   (2003) "Ecclesiology" in (ed) K.J. Vanhoozer The Cambridge Companion to Postmodern Theology. Cambridge: CUP, 252-68.

Harris P et al   (1994) Breaking New Ground: Church Planting in the Church of England. London: Church House Publishing.

Harvey BA   (1999) Another City. Harrisburg: Trinity Press International.

Hooker R   (1648) Of the Laws of Ecclesiastical Polity, as reproduced in modern language in (ed) A S McGrade (1989) Of the Laws of Ecclesiastical Polity Preface, Book I and Book VIII, Cambridge Texts in the History of Political Thought. Cambridge: CUP.

Horner R   (2005) Jean-Luc Marion A Theo-logical Introduction. Aldershot: Ashgate.

Jamieson A   (2002) A Churchless faith. London: SPCK.

Johnson S   (2001) Emergence. London: Penguin.

Karlsen JI   (1991) "Action Research as Method" in (ed) W Foote Whyte Participatory Action Research. London: Sage Publications, 143-58.

Langrish J   (1993) Case Studies as a Biological Research Process: Research Paper 67. Manchester: Institute of Advanced Studies, Manchester Metropolitan University.

Larson B, Osbourne R (1970) The emerging church. London: Word Books.

Leech K   (1997) The Sky is Red, Discerning the signs of the times. London: DLT.

Lynch G	(2000) After Religion. London: DLT.
Lyon D	(2002) Jesus in Disneyland. Oxford: Polity Press.
Maggay M	(1994) Transforming Society. Oxford: Lynx.
May T	(1993) Social Research: Issues, Methods and Process. Birmingham: Open University Press.
McCarthy M	(1999) "Spirituality in a Postmodern era" in Woodward J Pattison S A Blackwell Reader in Pastoral & Practical Theology. Oxford: Blackwell, 192-205.
McLaren B	(2004) A Generous Orthodoxy. Grand Rapids: Zondervan.
Millbank J	(1990) Theology and Social Theory: Beyond Secular Reason. Oxford: Blackwell.
Murray S	(2004) Church after Christendom. Carlisle: Paternoster Press.
Murray S	(2004) Post-Christendom, Church and Mission in a Strange New Land. Carlisle: Paternoster Press.
Murray S	(2005) "Rethinking atonement after Christendom" in Barrow S Bartley J Consuming Passion, Why the killing of Jesus really matters. London: DLT.
Palmer PJ	(1983) The Company of Strangers, Christians and the renewal of America's Public Life. New York: Crossroad.
Partridge C	(2005) "Alternative Spiritualities, Occulture and the Re-enchantment of the West" in The Bible in Translation, Summer 2005. Swindon: Bible Society.
Percy M	(2000) Introducing Richard Hooker and the Laws of Ecclesiastical

Polity. London: DLT.

Percy M   (1998) Power and the Church: Ecclesiology in an Age of Transition.
                   London: Continuum.

Percy M   (2002) The Salt of the Earth: Religious resilience in a Secular Age.
                   London: Continuum.

Porter A (ed)   (2003) The Imperial Horizons of British Protestant Missions, 1880-
                   1914, Studies in the history of Christian Missions. Cambridge:
                   Eerdmans Publishing Company.

Riddell M   (1998) God's home page. London: Bible Reading Fellowship.

Riddell M   (1998) Threshold to the Future. London: SPCK.

Rollins PJ   (2004) His Colour is Our Blood: A phenomenological of the prodigal
                   Father. A PhD thesis. Belfast: Queen's University.

Shanks A   (2000) God and Modernity, a new and better way to do theology.
                   London: Routledge.

Taylor S   (2005) A New Way of Being Church: A Case Study Approach
                   to Cityside Baptist Church as Christian Faith 'making do' in a
                   Postmodern World. A Doctorate Thesis. Dunedin, New Zealand:
                   University of Otago.

Taylor S   (2005) The out-of-bounds church? Learning to create communities
                   of faith in a culture of change. Grand Rapids, USA: Zondervan.

Thompson R   (1997) Is there an Anglican Way? Scripture, Church and Reason:
                   New Approaches to an Old Triad. London: DLT.

Timmis S (ed)   (2000) Multiplying Churches, Reaching Today's Communities Through
                   Church Planting. Fearn, Ross-Shire: Christian Focus Publishing.

Toyne P et al   (2004) A Measure for Measures: In mission and ministry. Report of the Review of the Dioceses, Pastoral Measure and related Measures. London: Church House Publishing.

Volf M   (1998) After Our Likeness The Church as the Image of the Trinity. Cambridge: Eerdmans.

Walker A   (1998) Restoring the Kingdom. The Radical Christianity of the House Church Movement. Guildford: Eagle.

Ward P   (2002) Liquid Church. Carlisle: Pater Noster Press.

Ward P (ed)   (2004) The Rite Stuff. Oxford: BRF.

Warren R   (1995) Being Human Being Church. London: Marshall Pickering.

Williams R   (2000) Lost Icons Reflections on Cultural Bereavement. London: T&T Clark.

Williams R   (2003) Presidential Address at General Synod, York Monday 14th July 2003, as retrieved 18th August 2005 from the World Wide Web, "http://www.archbishopofcanterbury.org/sermons_speeches/2003/030714.html".

Wood J   (2000) The Naomie Planning Model. Chingford: Youth work Central, as retrieved 3rd Septmber 2004 from the World Wide Web, "http://youthworkcentral.tripod.com/naomie.htm".

LaVergne, TN USA
03 May 2010
181304LV00002B/5/P